march 19, 1999

Allegra Taylor was born in 1940 and had an unconventional, globe-trotting childhood with no formal education. At seventeen she married film-maker Richard Taylor and they now have six grown-up children, two of whom they adopted while living in Nigeria and one in Kenya. They also have four grandchildren.

While the children were young, she took a degree in music and education and spent many years teaching music in her local community. She is also a freelance journalist.

She is a cancer survivor and a practising spiritual healer – a full member of The National Federation of Spiritual Healers.

TUTTLE ALTERNATIVE HEALTH

HEALING HANDS

by Allegra Taylor

Illustrated by Benedict Taylor

Charles E. Tuttle Company, Inc.
Boston • Rutland, Vermont • Tokyo

First published in the United States in 1993
by Charles E. Tuttle Company, Inc. of Rutland, Vermont
and Tokyo, Japan with editorial offices at
153 Milk Street, Boston, Massachusetts 02109

ISBN 0–8048–1832–0

Library of Congress Catalog Card Number 93–60273

00 99 98 97   3 5 7 9 10 8 6 4

Cover art by Isabelle Groblewski
Cover design by Fahrenheit

Printed in Singapore

CONTENTS

Preface		ix
Acknowledgments		xi
Chapter 1	Healing	1
Chapter 2	How To Find A Healer	14
Chapter 3	Working With Energy	26
Chapter 4	How To Develop Your Own Healing Powers	43
Chapter 5	The Use Of The Senses	59
Chapter 6	Looking After Your Body	86
Chapter 7	Some Healing Remedies For Common Ailments	97
Chapter 8	The Power of Love	118
Further Reading		135
Index		138

PREFACE

Very little of this material is entirely original. It is a distillation of some of the philosophical thoughts and practical ideas which I have learned on my own healing journey. It is a never-ending journey and I learn something new every day as doors keep opening onto bigger rooms, beckoning me further and further on.

It is hard to separate what is me from what are my sources. My teachers have been many and varied, and at the end I include a list of books which have been inportant to me. However, the truly extraordinary thing about the truth is that whenever you hear it you know instantly that you have always known it. Discovery is a process of remembering – being made whole.

ACKNOWLEDGMENTS

Many people have helped me in the preparation of this book. To those who have been my teachers and to those who have entered the sacred healing space with me I offer my love and thanks.

In particular I would like to thank healers Fauzia Said, Soozi Holbeche, Del Ralph, Craig Brown, Brue Richardson, Michael Dibdin, David Hadda, Don Copland, Sue Beechey, Dhyan Sutorius, Trudi Iles, Dan Benor, Alix Berlin, Jan de Vries, and Jean Sayre-Adams.

Thanks also to Harriet Griffey and Melissa Brooks for their helpful comments and suggestions, and to my family for their constant support and encouragement.

1
HEALING

A human being is part of the whole, called by us
'Universe', a part limited in time and space. He experiences his thoughts and feelings as something separated
from the rest, a kind of optical delusion of his consciousness. This delusion is a kind of prison for us, restricting
us to our personal desires and to affection for a few
persons nearest to us. Our task must be to free ourselves
from this prison by widening our circle of compassion to
embrace all living creatures and the whole of nature in
its beauty. Nobody is able to achieve this completely,
but the striving for such achievement is, in itself, a part
of the liberation and a foundation for inner security.

Albert Einstein

The human potential for transmitting energies of a healing nature has had many names through the centuries,
including the laying-on-of-hands, spiritual healing, faith
healing, magnetic healing, psychic healing and, more recently, in an attempt to make it sound more acceptable,
theraputic touch. In recorded history there is plenty of
evidence for the laying-on-of-hands being practiced in the
ancient civilizations of Egypt, Greece and Rome. The Chinese have been doing it since 5000 BC. In the Bible there
are several references to it and many of the miraculous
healings by Jesus were done by precisely this technique.
'These things that I do, so ye can do and more,' said Jesus,
which ought to give us the courage to try it.

Healing is taken for granted in many societies (or the
remnants of them) all over the world. The Native Americans, the Australian Aborigines, and European peas-
ant cultures are just a few societies that have
developed complex traditions of folk medicine of which

1

hand healing plays an integral part. We are only now rediscovering what people in more primary cultures have never really lost, that not only human beings but all living creatures are connected to one another another in some mysterious way and respond miraculously to the energy generated by love and care.

At the annual Festival of Mind, Body and Spirit in London, the largest crowd by far is to be found thronging the stand of the National Federation of Spiritual Healers where a constant succession of their volunteer healer members are on duty to cope with the huge demand.

This reflects the gathering groundswell of interest in healing and alternative therapies in recent years. Over a million people a year in Britain consult healers and there has been a significant growth in the healing ministeries in the church. It all indicates a widespread shift in the way we think about health; we are now much more inclined to acknowledge the connection between mind, body and spirit in maintaining a balanced, harmonious whole.

Twenty years ago Dolores Krieger, a professor of nursing in New York, became intrigued by the claims of a healer working in the United States and decided to put these claims to the test scientifically. One of her discoveries was that there was a significant increase in levels of haemoglobin in the blood of patients treated by laying-on-of-hands. Haemoglobin is the constituent in the blood responsible for transporting oxygen to the cells and tissues of the body. Convinced that anybody could be taught to do this, she evolved a method of teaching healing to nurses for them to practise in addition to their conventional nursing skills. She called this approach to healing 'therapeutic touch' so as not to frighten people off.

Since those pioneering days thousands of nurses and other health care professionals have been taught how to do therapeutic touch, with premature babies, with the terminally ill, with drug overdose cases, with post-operative patients, and astonishing results are now almost commonplace. Patients generally feel calmer, happier, more secure and less fearful. At the same time their own immune response improves, making them better able to help themselves. A doctor, James Lynch, Professor of Psychology at the University of Maryland's School of Medicine, has demonstrated that even the most simple forms of human contact, such as a nurse holding a patient's hand, have a dramatic beneficial effect on the body, especially the heart.

The effects of a calm, loving touch can be assessed: feelings of anxiety, hostility, pain and tension subside, blood pressure is stabilized, breathing becomes less shallow, heart rate and pulse slow down, and there are marked changes in hormone and haemoglobin levels in the blood. The person's energy, physical stamina and self-esteem improve.

The basic assumption in healing is that human beings are *open* systems, into and out of which flow constant streams of energy, producing an equilibrium and a symmetry in the body. Illness, from this viewpoint is, as many cultures have defined it, an imbalance in that symmetry, a blockage in the flow of energy.

Attempts to find scientific explanations for the power of healing have been only partly successful to date, as we don't yet possess adequate understanding, terminology or even means for measuring the phenomena. Because we are dealing with evidence that cannot easily be tested scientifically, healing is still regarded with immense suspicion by some rational thinkers, and many healers by trying to attribute half-baked scientific explanations to healing leave themselves wide open to ridicule.

However, most healers are in agreement that a force akin to biomagnetic or bioelectrical energy is being transmitted either through their hands directly to the person seeking help or through their mind in the case of absent healing when the patient is not present.

Philip Larkin, in his beautiful poem *Faith Healing*, wrote:

In everyone there sleeps
A sense of life lived according to love.

> To some it means the difference they could make
> By loving others, but across most it sweeps
> As all they might have done had they been loved.

Perhaps most disease is exacerbated by lack of love and companionship. If so, then one can assume that the reverse would be true – that healing is enabled and enhanced through the energy generated by love and care. This is not a new idea of course. Great teachers have been trying to help us understand this simple truth for a long time. One of its greatest exponents was Jesus himself, and his example remains a shining light.

History is filled with instances that demonstrate how kindly human contact acts as one of nature's most powerful antidotes to stress. There is a quality about love and companionship in life-threatening situations, such as war, concentration camps, severe illness or danger, that strengthens the body's biological and psychological power. In studies of cardio-vascular disease it has been proved that lack of human love can severely disturb the human heart and also, clearly, the reverse would be true. The presence of human love and care can serve as a powerful therapeutic force helping the heart to restore itself.

WHY IS IT CALLED SPIRITUAL HEALING?

It might be worth mentioning now that spiritual healing has nothing to do with spiritualism. The latter involves attempting to make contact with the spirits of people who have already died. Spiritual healing is so called because it acknowledges that we are more than the bodies we inhabit, that our essential being is a questing soul, a spirit whose search is for truth and wholeness, for homecoming. Leaving the spirit out of the equation is like trying to bake bread without any yeast. It gives us our wings and enables us to fly to a place where anything is possible.

The great advantage of spiritual healing over conventional Western scientific medicine is that it recognizes the spiritual dimension of our existence as the animating energy that holds everything else in balance. As Richard Moss has said, 'Healing eludes definition. No sooner is it grasped than it dissolves. It is a ceaseless process of relationship and discovery moment by moment. The more we "know" about healing the more we are carried toward the unknowable. For this reason all healing is, in essence, spiritual.'

Healing, like love, like birth, is both simple and extraordinary, both commonplace and miraculous. I have always rather resisted the terms spiritual healing or faith healing because of the implication that a particular religious belief is a necessary precondition for the healing process. Healing, of course, works regardless of belief and often without any faith in it at all on the part of the patient, as can be seen when it is used with very young children, animals or mentally handicapped people, for example.

In our predominantly secular society the 'spiritual' component of healing can pose a problem. All the healers I've ever come across believe that there is more to disease and health than the mere servicing of spare parts. All healers, whatever their belief system, describe the feeling of being a vessel, a conduit through which this healing energy flows. Something divine or cosmic or collective or perhaps just electrical, which transcends the frailty of its human channel. 'We are simply the conduit of the Divine Plan,' says Greek healer the Magus of Strovolos, in Kyriacos C. Markides's book of the same name. 'Success is not in our hands and we must resist the egotistical tendency to expect cure wherever we lay our hands. All we can do is try to help.'

The energy that activates another human being's failing recuperative powers of 'life-force' has been called unconditional love (or unconditional positive regard, if you prefer; love is still rather a four-letter word in some circles!). It is non-judgemental and compassionate. By creating a channel through which this loving energy flows, by acting rather like a 'jump lead', a healer can speed up, sometimes to an astonishing degree, the revitalizing process.

All healers understand the extraordinary potent energy generated by love and care and all healing techniques are aimed at balancing, amplifying and stimulating the natural flow of energies. It is eventually through opening the heart and giving love without judgement, without fear and without looking for results that miracles occur. The Greek word *energeia* from which our word 'energy' is derived was also the New Testament word for 'spiritual'.

ISN'T IT JUST 'ALL IN THE MIND'?

In our society we are rather quick to condemn anything 'in the mind' as being somehow illusory – at best hypnosis or brainwashing, at worst pathetic wishful thinking. We are wary of being duped or of kidding ourselves. Instead we should focus on how to harness the considerable creative mental powers we all possess.

One of the most effective ways to restructure ourselves is by using our imagination. This is a communication with an inner resource. In the Tibetan world view, for example, the line between real and imaginary is very soft focus indeed. Anything in the mind is as real as anything in front of your eyes and miracles are merely the clever handling of little known forces.

Perhaps 'trust' would be a better word to use than 'faith' when it comes to healing. In a state of trust it becomes possible to relax the usual defences and allow change to happen. For the patient to trust the healer is the most important prerequisite. Then together, they can surrender to the innate intelligence of the human organism and its urge to heal itself where possible, all other things being equal. Healers prepare themselves for a healing session by entering a calm and centred state of being. It is an attunement process which will heighten their own sensitivity to the patient's needs and create an inner rapport. This goes a long way towards establishing a trusting environment in which the patient can relax and let go.

Even so, the abstract quality of faith in itself, as demonstrated by the placebo effect or strong religious belief, is not to be despised. It can be a very useful tool for boosting the immune system or for anything else you might want to achieve. Thought is an extremely powerful creator and many healers use visualization and mental images to assist the healing process. As one healer said, 'The mind is the strongest tool we possess.'

Suggestion and auto-suggestion are vital, often necessary, conditions for change. The state of our health is after all inextricably connected to our thoughts and emotions. Doubt, pessimism and scepticism are powerful negative emotions that retard recovery. They are like putting a spell on yourself. The ancient intuitive healing arts work on the principle that the mind can activate or boost the body's immune system by an act of will, by mobilizing the life-force. We still work with this same principle today.

As Dr Daniel Benor, founder of the Doctor/Healer Network, points out, the lack of a sound theoretical foundation for healing has made it difficult for the medical profession to take it seriously as anything other than a placebo. Yet it is impossible to ignore the mounting body of evidence demonstrating healing effects at various levels from enzymes, cells, yeasts, bacteria to plants and animals which strongly points to factors other than mere suggestion.

After all, ultrasound, microwaves, X-rays and lasers are examples of energy frequencies we would never have believed possible a hundred years ago. Perhaps we should learn from such lessons and not be hasty in dismissing the even more subtle energies with which healers work until we have developed instrumentation of sufficient delicacy to measure them. Just because we don't know how something works doesn't mean that it can't work. One day we may understand more about how healing works but essentially, like life itself, it remains a mystery.

THE MYSTICAL ELEMENT

The undeniable fact remains, despite the attempts of our materialistic, secular society to undermine it, that human beings are complex creatures made up of physical, mental and spiritual dimensions. When they fall ill, it seems obvious, therefore, that it is the whole person who needs treatment. Healing is based on the premise that this whole person is more than a machine and more than the sum of its parts. An exploration of healing must also involve the unknown, not only the hidden agendas of old emotional baggage that we all carry, but also our connection to the sacred and to the magical. A person on a healing journey is like a mythic voyager bringing back his riches, carrying back what he has learned 'within' into outer 'reality', into daily life.

This notion of 'inner travel' is beset by prejudice. The common belief is that it is the preserve of weirdos, hippies or old ladies named Maud who sit in shuttered parlours smelling of furniture polish and moth-balls crying, 'Is there anybody there?' into the ether. But the nature of the spirit is to be free, to travel, to learn. The only structures that hold it trapped are our intellectual lobster pots which say, 'It isn't rational, it isn't logical, it can't be proved.' As the philosopher William James once said, 'Our normal waking consciousness is but one type of consciousness whilst all around it, parted from it by only the filmiest of screens, there lie potential forms of consciousness entirely different.'

Nowadays, because of the power of the experimental method, we have become brainwashed into believing that quantitative science is the shrine of ultimate knowledge. Yet an important part of the reality of our lives consists of just those things that are illusory or immeasurable. Not everything can be reduced to repeatable experiments, least of all the life of colours and sounds, pleasures and pains, ambitions, purposes and dreams. Healing may have more to do with a person's purpose and destiny, joy and appetite for life than things we can measure.

Philippa Pullar in her book, *Spiritual and Lay Healing*, says, 'One of the most important tasks of a healer is to get the patient's rational mind out of the way. By relaxing deeply and entering what is sometimes called an altered state of consciousness, his higher self, or his super-consciousness, can take over and do what is necessary to promote healing. The healer's role is to link the patient to and establish his relationship with his own source.'

SELF-HEALING

It has been said that all healing is really self-healing and to a great extent this is true. No healer can impose healing on any one. It is a conspiracy of emotional consent. Perhaps the best analogy is the one of the patient as bold adventurer travelling through difficult terrain and the healer as friend, helper and guide – not a magician but a catalyst. Then the healing process can be seen as a time to let go of old patterns of response, old coping strategies and old defence mechanisms, and as a new willingness to face the considerable challenge of the unknown.

An integral part of healing is the taking of personal responsibility on the part of the patient, with conscious committment to change. A healer is there to help create the space in which that dynamic change can take place. A lot of pain and disease is formed by attitudes. Not all illness comes from outside ourselves; often it has roots in our inner being. An illness is the result not only of mechanical failure or exposure to an infectous agent but also of the inability of a person's immune system to protect him against the intruder. Depression, lack of a feeling of basic self-worth, fear, anxiety and loneliness all contribute to a weakening of the immune response.

So much of illness arises as a defence against life – the line of least resistance – where it can become almost a relief to give up the fight. Gradually dismantling the defences means allowing the life-force to flow in. This is where trust comes in, not to mention a great deal of courage and determination. Being healthy is quite hard work. Good health is much more than an absence of disease. It is an embracing of life. Clearly, to be able to receive is as important as to be able to give. If you are not receptive, whether to an energy or an idea, it will pass you by.

The 'holistic' concept puts a large measure of responsibility and participation into the hands of the patient. A disease is of a damaged person not just a damaged part. We are encouraged to look beyond the symptoms and ask, 'What do I use illness for?' 'What is it telling me about myself and the way I lead my life?' 'Why this disease rather than another?' and perhaps the hardest and most profound question of all, 'If I could get rid of this illness, what would I put in its place?'

In the summer of 1989 I was diagnosed as having cancer and even in the midst of the shock and trauma, I felt a great sense of awe for the brilliance of my body in having found a way to alert me in time. But to what? Part of my healing would lie with the job of finding out which patterns of behaviour, which coping strategies in my life were screaming at me, 'Change or die!'

I knew that I would have to work with the cancer rather than against it in order to hear more clearly what it was trying to tell me and to make sense of it. The important thing was that the cancer was me. My body had manifested it for some reason which had nothing to do with guilt or blame or punishment. I certainly do not believe that I must have deserved it and that is why I got it, but I saw it as a *process* and a metaphor. If I had made it, then I could understand what it was doing there and I could make it go away.

This revelation changed me instantly from a hapless, helpless victim into a participant in my own healing. When your life has seemingly been overtaken by catastrophe you feel very powerless. Getting back in the driving seat again is an essential part of the recovery process.

The course of action that I chose was to have the surgery and radiotherapy recommended by my consultant and to augment the expertise of the medical profession with everything I could possibly do to help myself. Going to a healer was an essential part of this holistic approach. Under her gentle, intuitive touch, I surrendered myself into the hands of the universe and asked to be able to open myself so that the healing energy could flow into me. I felt I was transcending the personal and plugging into the collective. It was a wonderful, relaxed feeling, almost joyful. Together with some dietary changes and a course of acupuncture, I was content that I was doing the best I could for myself to counter the brutal assault of the orthodox treatment while, at the same time, acknowledging how grateful I was for the skill and experience of my doctors.

I could feel all the tensions, toxins and blockages slowly drain away, leaving me refreshed, peaceful and tranquil. I was healing not just at the physical level, but at the emotional and spiritual levels too. The healing took the whole of me into account, not just the illness from which I was recovering, but the context in which it had occurred – the me that is still a little child, the me that is still full of fears and anxieties, the me that is growing up, the me that's trying to make sense of my life. None of this was to do with guilt, only compassion.

Of course I didn't 'choose' to be ill at a conscious level, but a wiser part of me may have known it was the only way to make me take stock. Now that it's happened I feel grateful for how much I have learned.

THE LIFE-FORCE

You will hear a lot about the life-force in any discussions on healing. It is an attempt to describe the concept of an energy flow in the body. In other words, it is the unique, energetic, vitalizing substance that flows from the environment into the body. It arrives at the moment of conception and departs at the moment of death. In the Hindu tradition it is known as 'prana', the subtle energy within sunlight that is assimilated through the breath. The Chinese concept is called 'ch'i' and is seen as a nourishing vital energy which permeates our environment and is distributed throughout the body via a network of meridians. Blockages and weaknesses which arise for whatever reason – physical, emotional, spiritual – and cause an interruption in the free-flowing nature of this energy are the cause of much 'dis-ease'. The healer's main objective is to facilitate, by the warmth and gentleness of non-judgemental loving touch, the restoration and re-balancing of this energy.

HEALING AND THE MEDICAL PROFESSION

Ted Kaptchuk and Michael Croucher in their book *The Healing Arts* wrote: 'By its very nature any medicine is only partial; a mirror of the people who created it – an expression of what they thought about themselves or believed about their world. The medicine of the scientific tradition is a powerful one, but it reflects our limitation to an analytical view of the world that ignores many other facets of life.'

They go on to put forward a model of integrated medicine in which practitioners of distinctly different healing arts could co-operate with one another in a multi-dimensional approach. There is no single invincible system that can tackle illness in all its complex and paradoxical manifestations, so it's a good idea to give each its due and be prepared to consider the whole range of healing systems that the genius of the human race has worked out so patiently.

Unfortunately, due to the polarity and mistrust between medicine and healing, a lot of people who come to healers only do so as a last resort, when high-tech scientific medicine has been unable to help them and all else has failed. By this time they are chronically ill and desperate. Instead of seeing healing as a wonderful *complementary* therapy to be used alongside the best that Western scientific medicine can offer, it is seen as a desperate alternative.

A shadow of fear still surrounds the idea of healing

because of the appalling persecution during the time of the Inquisition of 'sorcerers' and 'witches' – usually midwives and herbalists – in the name of religion. The Church claimed a monopoly of gifts of the spirit and any lay person who attempted to heal was accused of being in league with the devil and put to death. Incredibly the witchcraft laws were still on the statute books until 1953, and even today Christian fundamentalists have been known to disrupt healers' meetings declaring all healing not connected with the church to be diabolic.

Fortunately this is slowly beginning to change, largely due to the sterling endeavors of the non-denominational National Federation of Spiritual Healers who for thirty years have worked calmly and tirelessly to present an unsensational, acceptable, commonsensical image of healing. Their members, who have served long apprenticeships as probationary healers and are bound by a strict Code of Ethics, are now welcomed in most hospitals whenever a patient has requested their services. A wise physician will mobilize every possible healing resource as well as help patients to mobilize their own resources.

A healer should always ask you what treatment or medical advice you have been given by your doctor and you will not be asked to alter it. Healing is a totally non-invasive therapy and can't possibly do any harm. It works at a very subtle level, like sunshine on plants, creating a favourable environment in which cells can regenerate. Even in situations where cure is not a realistic objective, healing helps greatly to improve the quality of life.

2
HOW TO FIND A HEALER

If you think healing might be something you would like to try, your next task is to find a healer. Many people are worried by tales of exploitation and charlatanism, which can be particularly upsetting at a time when they are feeling vulnerable. Personal recommendation is one of the best ways to track down a healer. Otherwise trust your instinct. If a person makes you feel uneasy or guarded, they are not for you. Not all healers will suit everyone and compatability is important. There may be a healing centre near you offering counselling and self-help groups as well as a variety of healing techniques. Don't be afraid to shop around. It's important for you to feel happy with your choice.

WHAT ABOUT COST?

Healers remain divided on the thorny question of what to charge for their services. Some maintain that it is wrong to charge anything for exercising a God-given gift, although it stands to reason that if a healer has no other source of income and is devoting all her time to healing, she must be expected to earn a living. After all, a teacher or a pianist or a linguist is also exercising a God-given gift. I think I agree with the late great Scottish healer, Bruce MacManaway, who said that anyone believing himself or herself to be a healer should be careful about charging to begin with, but, once satisfied of the power to help others, should feel justified in earning a living from those endeavours.

stands to reason that if a healer has no other source of income and is devoting all her time to healing, she must be expected to earn a living. After all a teacher or a pianist or a linguist is also exercising a God-given gift. I think I agree with the late great Scottish healer, Bruce MacManaway, who said anyone believing himself or herself to be a healer should be careful about charging to begin with, but, once satisfied of their power to help others, should feel justified in earning a living from those endeavours.

It is difficult to give even an average cost of a session with a healer. Much depends on the level of training the practitioner has. For example, a physician who uses healing touch in practice will charge more than someone who simply believes in the treatment and sets up practice without scientific schooling. And again, much depends on whether or not the healer's practice is the sole source of income. Many healers still give their services for free or ask for a voluntary donation. It would be rare for a healer to turn anyone away who couldn't afford much, and many will adjust their fees or be willing to barter. One man who used to come to me for healing always brought some produce from his allotment, another did some painting and decorating. The point is, it's negotiable and nobody should feel barred from healing because of financial hardship.

In addition, more and more people are wanting to learn some basic healing skills for themselves in order to help family and friends in times of need, and I explore this further in Chapter 4.

THE FIRST CONSULTATION – WHAT TO EXPECT

When going to a healer, it's important to see the work you are going to do together as a partnership. There is no simple answer to the question, 'Who is doing the healing?' As was said earlier, it is a conspiracy of emotional consent. In allowing this to take place you are creating the conditions for the life-force to flow in and do its work. As American doctor, Rachel Naomi Remen, has said, 'I don't believe that one person heals another; I believe that what we do is invite the other person into a healing relationship. We heal together.'

Healing is a very individual event and each healer will have his or her own style. Some combine the healing with counselling, particularly in the case of emotional problems, providing people with the opportunity to talk about the things in their lives that they are seeking to change.

The healer will have prepared himself for you by getting into a calm and centred state and creating a safe and peaceful atmosphere. Many healers start by offering a prayer for guidance and ask to be used as a channel for healing energy. If you like the idea, that might be something you could do together. I have one young patient with AIDS and we begin all our sessions like that at his suggestion. I never cease to feel awed by the sacred nature of the healing space. It is a crucible of transformation and deserves to be approached in a state of great humility and wonder.

You will probably be asked to sit in a chair or lie on a treatment table (I often treat people on the floor). You will not be asked to remove any clothing except your shoes. There may be crystals, candles or soft soothing music to aid relaxation. The healer will usually then do a brief scan of your energy field just to see what useful clues he can pick up. Disturbances or deficits might be felt by the healer as a wave of heat or coldness.

So much of the healing that follows depends upon the healer's intuitive knowledge of where to place his hands,

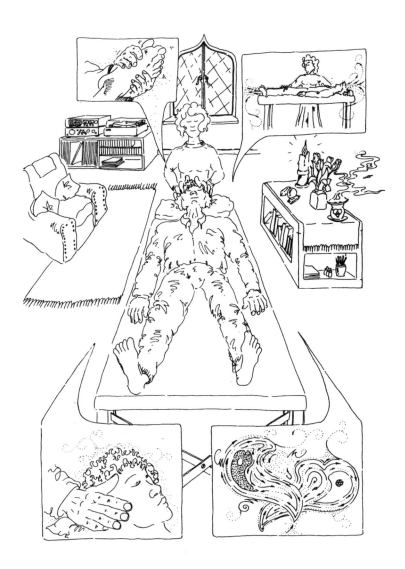

Fig. 1 Creating a healing environment

and there is no set formula. I might focus my attentions on a particular trouble spot, say a wound or a scar. I might invite the patient to breathe deeply and visualize with me a colour associated with a depleted chakra (see pp. 26–32). I might work my way around the whole body doing a general energy balancing, connecting up the chakras by placing my hands on each one in turn and imagining a current of pure white light running through them from top to bottom. I might focus on the feet if I feel a person needs 'grounding'. If a person is very emotionally distressed I might synchronize my breathing with his and channel warmth into the abdomen or heart areas. I might work entirely on the head, just trusting that the healing energy will go wherever it is needed.

Many healers prefer to transmit energy through their hands without making actual physical contact, but I personally feel that in our alienated and touch-starved society the therapeutic effects of touch can be an important part of the healing. After many decades of increasingly depersonalized medical practices in the West, doctors are once again coming round to acknowledging that physical contact may be a decisive factor in vanquishing illness. The skin is, after all, the largest and most sensitive organ of the body.

There may be exceptions to this of course – in cases of extreme pain or where the patient feels very threatened, for example – and part of the healer's sensitivity includes being alert to the appropriateness of touch. Sometimes it can be introduced at a later stage. You should discuss this with your healer if you feel at all uncomfortable.

People can be 'touched' emotionally too, and one of the skills a healer needs is sto know how to reach out and find ways of touching people. This is all part of establishing the ambience of trust, safety and mutual respect that is essential to the healing process.

The very first time I ever encountered anything resembling a holistic approach was when, in desperation after many years of suffering migraine headaches, I was persuaded by a friend to visit an Indian osteopath and acupuncturist some years ago. He put his hands gently on the back of my shoulders and the first question he asked me was, 'What makes you angry?'

I could feel the tears welling up immediately. It was a revelation. No doctor had ever asked me anything about myself before, what I thought or felt. It set me thinking about the way I stored frustrations in my body. It seems so obvious now but he made me conscious for the first time in my life of all the contributory factors which finally manifest themselves as a symptom. A pill to take away the symptom may be tempting but is not the real answer unless it forms part of a wider strategy to unravel the cause.

If you are unable to get out, you should be able to find a healer who will pay you a home visit. Certainly you will be able to have absent or distant healing. Absent healing works just as well as contact healing although it seems hard to believe. The healer, at an appointed time, will 'tune in' to you and channel the healing energy in the same way. Since this energy is not restricted by the limitations of our usual concept of space and time it can travel anywhere, instantly with the speed of the healer's thoughts. Time and distance are no obstacle and the energy is at liberty to traverse any space and find communion with the person seeking healing (see Fig. 2).

If you are in a hospital and would like a healer to visit you, it would be a good idea to talk to your doctor and explain why you are taking this extra step to do everything you can to help yourself. Also, check with the nursing staff about how best to fit in with hospital routine. You may get a few funny looks but it's very rare these days to get an outright refusal.

I was recently called to the bedside of a young girl seriously injured in a road accident. The hospital chaplain and I joined forces and, each with our own frame of reference, sat on either side of her holding her hands and asked for God's healing energy to flow into her.

Fig. 2 Absent healing

HOW LONG DOES IT TAKE?

The average healing session takes anything from 20 minutes to an hour, although many healers prefer to do a very long session of up to three hours which includes plenty of time for talking. At the other end of the scale, it is possible to accomplish some amazing healing in a very short time. Years ago, before I had begun to explore my own healing potential, I was travelling on a train in Italy. A young man in the same carriage suddenly began having an asthma attack. Very calmly an elderly woman sitting in the opposite corner set down her basket and came across to him. 'I can help you if you will allow me,' she said, and put one hand on the front of his chest and the other on his back. 'Let me breathe for you,' she said and began a quiet, deep breathing rhythm. Within seconds the young man's panic subsided and he had matched his breathing to hers. The woman took out a big handkerchief and wiped his brow tenderly. She sat talking softly to him for the rest of the journey to make sure he was alright. This was a wonderful example of healing first-aid – heart-to-heart resuscitation.

WHAT DOES IT FEEL LIKE?

Many people report sensations of warmth or mild tingling when receiving healing, but it's not unusual to feel nothing at all. The healing works whether you feel anything or not. Often, like I myself did, people feel very tearful. Don't be ashamed of this, it is a good sign and very natural. It is such a relief to feel that you are heard. The most common reaction is just a lovely feeling of general relaxation. As the energy begins to flow into you, tensions will ease, breathing will become deeper, your hands and feet will probably feel warm and heavy. As the body functions slow down and become calm you may even feel that you are drifting off to sleep. This isn't really sleep as you are fully conscious and aware of your surroundings. You could hear if your healer spoke to you or if someone came into the room. It is actually a semi-hypnotic state of altered consciousness called the alpha state which refers to the brain wave pattern. It is the transitionary state between waking and sleeping that we all go through every night and morning.

A BIT MORE ABOUT BRAIN WAVES

Breathing techniques are at the heart of most teaching about healing. Healers can most effectively centre themselves and heighten their sensitivity to energy vibrations by paying attention to their breathing. It is the key to expanded capabilities. From a self-healing point of view, different breathing patterns cause a change in the brain waves enabling you to control and regulate such processes as heart rate, blood volume, temperature and pain relfexes.

Stress clinics in the United States have pioneered the use of biofeedback machines – wiring patients up to a little meter that monitors these changes, thereby teaching them to bring themselves consciously into a calmer state by breathing and relaxation. Some healers have even asked, 'Why stop there?', reasoning that we might also be able to influence malignant growths, infection and the regeneration of tissue and bone.

Consciousness expands with breathing. Jack Schwartz, the pioneer American healer, has categorized the brain wave breathing rhythm as follows:

Beta rhythm, at a frequency of 13–30 cycles per second. This is the normal waking rhythm associated with active, questioning linear thinking and concrete problem solving. It is a shallow, upper-chest breathing with a high-frequency, low-amplitude wave.

Alpha rhythm, at a frequency of 8–13 cycles per second. This is a relaxed passive rhythm associated with inwardly directed attention, meditation and feelings of contentment, like a cat with its purring. It is abdominal breathing with some diaphragmatic expansion.

Theta rhythm, at a frequency of 4–7 cycles per second. This frequency appears in dreaming, daydreaming and visualizations. It is lower abdominal breathing and is associated with access to the unconscious mind, deep meditation and creative inspiration.

Delta rhythm at $\frac{1}{2}$–4 cycles per second. Low-frequency, high-amplitude diaphragmatic breathing is associated with deep sleep and, paradoxically, with higher levels of consciousness and paranormal phenomena.

If you are operating purely on beta rhythms, you will be pretty much trapped in your skin, whereas theta waves reach way beyond the restrictions of time and space. You can learn to alter your brain wave rhythms by exhaling over a long count. Things like oxygen and glucose content in the blood alter dramatically, keeping negativity at bay and making you more receptive to a higher, finer quality of energy, encouraging a transpersonal state.
　Try this exercise:

Breathe in for 4 counts.
Hold for 4.
Breathe out for 4.
Pause for 4.
Repeat 3 times.

Now repeat 3 more times and try to lengthen the outbreath, to 8 counts, then 16, then 32.

WHAT CAN YOU DO TO HELP YOURSELF?

When we get ill there is an enormous temptation to hand over the responsibilty passively to someone else. We go to the doctor to fix us up, saying, 'I can't give up smoking, I don't want to change my diet, I'm too busy to take any time off, I hate exercise, don't ask me to give up the booze – my only recreation is having a few drinks with my friends. Just make me better.'

If you see going to a healer as an extension of this – a sort of lottery where you can hit the jackpot if you're lucky – the chances are not too good. A healer can only help you to the extent that you are committed to change. Illness is usually the result of a combination of internal and external factors. Depression, for instance, and other emotional disorders can cause a suppression of the body's natural defences against illness, leading to an increased susceptibility to the external agents of disease, such as viruses and bacteria.

We also waste a tremendous amount of our precious life-force energy by allowing a state of permanent tension to build up, causing high blood pressure, heart problems, stomach disorders and any number of joint and muscle pains, stiff necks, clenched jaws and headaches. Helping your doctor to help you means asking yourself some tough questions and doing what you can to affect the internal factors through proper diet, meditation, exercise, stress reduction techniques and any of the holistic therapies that appeal to you.

If you've chosen to come to a healer, you can greatly augment the benefit of the treatment by setting aside some time every day to practise relaxation, breathing and visualization (see page 34). There are many relaxation tapes available or you could use your favourite soothing music. I have a tape of ocean sounds combined with the songs of the humpback whale that sends me off into the realms of alpha every time without fail. Surrendering or dissolving into music is one of the best ways of opening the door and allowing yourself to walk out of the room full of all the clanking, whirring machinery of everyday pre-occupations into the sunlit uplands of limitless possibi-lities.

Openness, patience, awareness, willingness – these are the qualities you need for your epic journey to wholeness, for your mythic voyage. You need to be on the lookout for the metaphorical components of your illness. You need to consider your survival strategies and the ways in which you relate to other people. You need to face your fear of living life to the full. 'All diseases are labelled fear of change,' says Jack Schwartz. 'You need to be willing to take a few risks, come to grips with the anxiety of the possibility of loss, even of non-being. If you really let your-self go with the willingness to change and grow, you will expand and unfurl and there are no limits to what might come your way – maybe even miracles. Fear limits our ability to live freely.'

If we can approach our life and our healing from a perspective of courageous expectancy, any experience has within it the power to transform and heal.

3
WORKING WITH ENERGY

A human being is not entirely contained by his skin. One of the first leaps of new thinking is to be able to understand this bigger dimension which we inhabit. 'The vital force is not enclosed in man,' wrote Paracelsus in the sixteenth century, 'but radiates in and around him like a luminous sphere.' This three-dimensional energy field or aura, as it is called, envelops the body in a sort of incandescent pod of light, an etheric space suit, an iridescent chrysalis. It is part of our body but not dense enough to have become matter. The aura reflects, in a glow around your body, the sum total of your past experiences and your state of health. It is visible to people with highly developed perception who describe it as a multi-layered radiant cloud but most of us can't see it. It is easier to feel it or sense it and, with practice, healers can become very accurate in diagnosing areas of imbalance.

If we perceive healing as a rebalancing of the subtle energy fields that regulate the body, it's helpful to have some kind of mental picture of what is going on. The ancient Eastern concept of the *chakras* (a Sanskrit word meaning 'wheels') has been adopted as symbolic language by most holistic practitioners to describe the gateways or main points of entry by which energy can flow into and out of the body. They can be imagined as little dynamos or transformers, taking in higher energy and directing it to where it is needed. Acupuncture and shiatsu points are a more detailed and expanded version of this concept where the whole body is mapped out as a series of inter-connecting meridians or pathways.

In much the same way as the digestive system, for

example, takes in energy in the form of physical nutrients (ie food), the chakras, in conjunction with the acupuncture meridians, take in and distribute higher vibrational energies that are just as vital to the proper growth and maintenance of physical life. For a more detailed discussion of these concepts read Richard Gerber's exciting book, *Vibrational Medicine.*

Although we are limited to our five senses, they can be greatly expanded and made much more sensitive. Healers who have developed clairvoyant skills are able to see great whirling catherine wheels of colour where the chakras are situated and can tell at a glance if they are out of balance, deficient or overactive. I have to confess that I am not able to see auras myself, but I can feel where a person's energy is sluggish or blocked by scanning the chakras with my hands. To me, the chakras feel like pairs of cone-shaped vortices spiralling into the body both front and back. Illness always seems to be associated with a shut-down in the free-flowing nature of the energy which should stream through these portals. One way of regarding illness is to see it as stagnant energy; therefore the way to health begins with stirring it up.

As quantum physics has opened the windows onto unimaginable new landscapes where science and mysticism meet, spiritual healing has begun to advance on the wave of growing understanding that we are dealing with finer and subtler forms of energy than we ever thought possible. Areas where matter and energy become interchangeable, where consciousness and body come together, where all the mechanical ways in which we have described ourselves for far too long begin to seem terribly crude.

The basic law of life is motion – radiant, vibrant energy – and science is at last beginning to discover what mystics have always known, that matter itself is made up of this energy. That beyond molecules, atoms, protons, neutrons and electrons there are components that can no longer be characterized as matter but as waves or particles. In other words, all matter, however dense it may appear, can be seen as a constant dance of energy and although our bodies may appear to be solid and opaque, at the most fundamental level, we are made up of pure energy. This 'too, too solid flesh' of ours is not really solid at all and can be influenced by very subtle vibrations. The energy from the different chakras can be awakened and harmoniously balanced. Stagnant energy can be dispersed. The wellbeing of the physical body depends on this.

THE CHAKRAS

There are seven principal chakras ranged along the axis of the spine in a vertical line from the base to the top of the head (see Fig. 3). They are charged by energy from the sun in the form of light which enters the individual chakras at different vibrationary rates causing each one to resonate to a different colour of the spectrum. Once we can understand the idea that each of the chakras resonates with a particular vibrationary frequency that corresponds to a certain colour and sound, it is easier to understand how colour and sound, crystals, homoeopathic medicines and other forms of vibrational remedies can have a therapeutic effect.

Most of the so-called 'New Age' approaches to healing recognize that deficiencies in this subtle, invisible, elusive energy are a primary cause of illness, and they seek to redress the balance by harnessing the energy from plants (herbalism), from the essence of living flowers (Bach Flower Remedies), from crystals and gemstones, from sound and colour, and, perhaps most basic of all, from loving touch. All of these things have vibrational frequencies and work by sympathetic resonance. They can help fine-tune us when we are out of synch. The vibrational remedies offer us a set of tools to help mobilize the body's own self-healing abilties.

Think of the tuning dial of your radio. If it is a fraction of a millimetre off the correct frequency you get interference, disturbance, cacophony. A minute adjustment and all the flotsam and jetsam clear miraculously, leaving

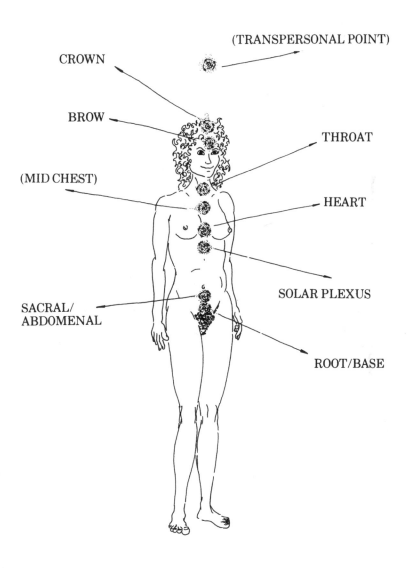

Fig. 3 The *chakras*

N.B. Not all healers agree precisely on the above locations.

you with a Mozart piano concerto or Ella Fitzgerald.

Each major chakra corresponds roughly, in our ordinary anatomical understanding, to the location of an endocrine gland and a major nerve plexus. Each one also governs a different part of the body and the particular physiological functions and life-issues associated with that part of the body.

First
At the bottom of the spine, near the coccyx, is the base or root chakra. It is the sexual or reproductive centre linked to the gonads – the germ gland; sperm and ovaries. Its colour is red, the colour of vitality, heat, passion – the fire in the basement.

Second
At the junction with the pelvic bone is the abdominal or sacral chakra. It is linked to the adrenals, the active 'fight or flight' centre. It governs the kidneys and the digestive process and its colour is orange, the colour of personal power, consciousness and mental energy.

Third
The solar plexus chakra is associated with the rational intellectual left side of the brain and is linked to the pancreas. It reflects disharmonies in the liver or spleen and its colour is yellow, the colour of the intellect.

Fourth
The heart chakra is our emotional centre. Its colour is green and it is linked to the thymus gland. It reveals how we relate to people and how much 'heart' we put into things. Interestingly, most people seem quite happy to accept this concept. The heart is well established in popular mythology as the place where we feel love, hate, grief or courage. We talk about being heartened, sick at heart, heartbroken. A person is described as hard-hearted, black-hearted, kind-hearted, lion-hearted, faint-hearted. According to recent research, the subtle energy flow

through the heart chakra may well prove to be crucial in the effective functioning of the thymus gland and therefore of the body's immune response.

Fifth
The throat chakra is linked to the thyroid, which regulates metabolism. It is associated with communication, both vocal and through the arms and hands. It takes care of the area of the neck and shoulders where many people carry an enormous amount of tension. Its colour is a light or turquoise blue, the colour of expressive energy, volitional authority.

Sixth
Indigo is the colour of the brow chakra, located in the area of the 'third eye', corresponding to the pituitary gland which influences growth of the body. This is the intuitive, non-verbal, creative right side of the brain associated with inner vision.

Seventh
Finally right on the top of the head is the crown chakra, often depicted in Hindu or Buddhist painting as a thousand-petalled lotus flower. Linked to the pineal gland, which some teachers of healing have likened to a prism – refracting and separating out the different colours from pure white light in order to send them to each individual chakra – this is our spiritual centre. From here we evolve our appreciation of art, religion and beauty and connect with out concept of God. Its colour is purple, the colour of wholeness, spirituality and integration. (Catholic cardinals wear amethyst rings.) Representations of Christian saints and angels show halos of golden light over the crown chakra signifying holiness or wholeness. This chakra, like the pineal gland, is to do with the receptivity of light in both the physical and the metaphysical sense.

Transpersonal Point
There is also, in some schools of thought, the Transpersonal Point which is seen as a small ball of energy 12 to

24 inches above the top of the head. It is represented by pure white light and refers to the collective, the out-of-the-body, the universal, the divine.

It's important to remember that all this is a poetic and symbolic representation of something we are still struggling to grasp. Most healers find the chakra system useful to borrow, as we in the West have no indigenous symbolic frame of reference. I use the concept of the chakras to help me focus and channel energy into the body.

You can also begin to see how adding a colour to the energy being channelled gives it an extra potency. A young woman with a chronic inflamed throat condition came to me for healing. Antibiotics would clear it up for a while, but it kept recurring and was at risk of jeopardizing her singing career. It transpired that she had always had a very trying relationship with her dominating, controlling mother and consequently felt that she had never been allowed to speak for herself. 'I'm crying out to just be me,' she said one day, providing with that graphic statement the main clue we needed. So I beamed the energy through my hands to her throat chakra while both of us visualized the colour of turquoise blue streaming through her body, simultaneously cooling the inflammation and revitalizing her centre of communication.

It proved to be a remarkable turning point and in only three sessions she 'found her voice' and the sore throats began to disappear of their own accord.

VISUALIZATION

If you can accept the obvious fact that the mind is the most effective tool we possess for bringing about the changes we want in our lives, then visualization is the art of harnessing that mental energy.

This is not as complicated as it sounds. We all do it unconsciously every day in hundreds of ways. If I stand in my garden on a winter's morning looking at the sleeping beds of bare earth, I can picture in my mind the moment when the spring bulbs will burst out of the earth filling my eyes with colour and my heart with pleasure. I can picture myself 5 lbs thinner, lying on a beach, trekking in Peru, sitting at a cafe table in Venice – anything I want, in fact – and the scene is set for me to put into action whatever steps are needed to realize my dream. Thought always precedes action even in something as simple as getting the milk from the fridge or crossing the road.

Visualization is learning to use this natural image-making capacity in a more conscious and deliberate fashion. In the same way that an architect will first make a drawing of the structure he is going to build, what you are doing, in fact, is creating a mental picture or blueprint of the state you want to bring about (peace, calm, healing of a broken bone, reduction of a tumour) and focussing positive energy on it. This simple technique is enormously helpful in marshalling our forces, dissolving our internal barriers and allowing the healing energy to do its work.

Children are born with this wonderful capacity to visualize, but instead of teaching them how to use it creatively we actively discourage it: 'Stop daydreaming!', 'Pay attention!', 'Head in the clouds again!', 'Always in a world of your own!', 'Don't make things up!' We forget that make-believe can become make-happen.

Having had our imaginations ridiculed as children we can sometimes find it difficult to kick start them again in later life. Don't worry if nothing seems to happen at first or you feel self-conscious; just leave yourself open to the idea. Set yourself some 'flash tasks' just to get in the habit. Picture a room in your house in as much detail as possible; picture the face of someone you love; think of a red silk scarf; imagine the taste of a lemon; a wood full of bluebells; the smell of fresh coffee; the texture of velvet or granite. See? You're doing it! (Incidentally, most people, although they may be reluctant to admit it, have plenty of imagination when it comes to sexual fantasies.)

Fig. 4 Visualization 'flash tasks'

How to start

Begin by lying down or sitting comfortably with your back supported. Breathe deeply, counting slowly backwards from 10. Then, working up the body beginning with your feet, tense and relax all your muscles so that you can really feel the difference. When you feel ready, gently begin to let your imagination off the leash.

One of the simplest and most effective ways to start is with a pure colour visualization. Imagine a wash of watercolour flooding down a piece of white paper, or a field of yellow daffodils, a blaze of autumn leaves, a market stall piled with oranges or a newly mown meadow green – any way you can think of to fill your mind with a single colour. If you can't 'see' it, try just to get a feel of it or a sense of it.

The next stage is to imagine your breath taking on a colour, softly whooshing in and out of your body, travelling just beneath the surface of your skin. Now you can target this colour to wherever you want it to go. Just breathe it into a needy or depleted part of your body. Visualize blue if you need calming, red if you need warming, yellow if you need cheering.

Shirley Maclaine in one of her books tells the story of finding herself in a mountain hut in Tibet one freezing cold night with nothing but the thin clothes she was wearing. Knowing that her chances of survival would be pretty slim unless she could persuade her body that it was somewhere else, she closed her eyes and visualized a big yellow sun shining down on her. She stopped shivering and fell asleep basking in the warmth of her imagination and astounded everyone by suffering no ill effects.

When I was undergoing radiation treatment for my cancer, I tried something similar. I remembered reading years ago about some experiments in which volunteer subjects under hypnosis were told they were going to have hot wax dripped on to their skin. Instead they were touched lightly with a pencil, but a blister appeared just the same. I reasoned that if I could fill my mind with images of fresh cold water while I was, in fact, being bombarded with burning killer rays, I should be able to 'persuade' my skin not to blister. So I created foaming cascades, mountain streams, crashing breakers, forest pools where I cavorted and splashed. I found I could even make myself shiver and give myself goosebumps. At the end of the eight weeks of daily treatment I hadn't burnt at all, although I am very fair skinned, and the whole area healed remarkably quickly.

Every achievement starts first in the imagination, and you already have everything you need at your fingertips just waiting to be used. So allow yourself to experiment. The American poet Emerson once said, 'What lies behind us and what lies before us are small matters compared to what lies within us.'

Some ideas

Here are a few of my favourite visualizations. Change them in any way you like or, better still, throw out mine and make up your own. Sometimes I suggest them to clients who come for healing as an inner journey we can take together. Sometimes I just do them myself when I need to relax. When you have chosen your theme, take it slowly, one step at a time, leaving about a minute between each new idea as it appears, spending approximately 20–30 minutes in total on your creation.

All of them start in the same way: getting into a warm, comfortable position sitting or lying down, breathing deeply and slowly counting backwards from 10, tensing and relaxing all the muscles beginning from the feet up....

The underwater sea cave
Picture the entrance to a sunlit rocky cove where the sea is lazily swelling and falling against rocks. It is a safe, protected place where you come to sit on the white sandy beach. There is a delicious fresh salty tang in the air, the sun is warm on your back. A slight breeze ruffles your hair and your toes enjoy the feeling of the fine, silvery sand. What can you see? ... Some beautiful shells? ... A dolphin leaping in the bay? ... A couple of sailing boats on the horizon? ... A pair of sea birds nesting on the cliff? ... Feast your eyes. What can you hear? ... A seagull's cry? ... The water gently lapping the shore? ... The sound of your own breathing? ... What can you smell? ... The sea? ... The sun on your skin? ... Lie down for a while and close your eyes. Let your other senses do the work. See with your inner eyes.

You will feel too relaxed to move a muscle, so instead of going for a swim you make believe that you are a piece of seaweed floating just inside the entrance to an underwater sea cave. The water is a translucent aquamarine and the perfect temperature. Each time the sea swells the water rushes into the cave and you are lifted and carried. Your branches are hollow and the sea-green water pours through them filling them with vitality. You are alive, the sea is alive, the planet is alive. You are one. The Earth is breathing.

With every in-breath you are filled with life. Sunlight and sea water rush through your veins bringing healing, and peace, acceptance and forgiveness. With every outbreath you let go of all the tensions and blockages that have served their purpose. Feel the toxins drain away. All pains and fears float out of your body. You are in your very first element both in this lifetime and in the whole history of life on Earth.

You are permeated by the colour of the sea which flows in and out through every orifice, through every extremity. ... Sparkling, blue-green, effervescent, invigorating. The gentle energy that can wear away the hardest rock and rust the toughest iron will cleanse you. Know that you are held in the arms of Mother Earth and all the healing properties of sea water are here for you whenever you need them. Know that you can return here at any time.

Slowly come out of your reverie on the shore. Fix this wonderful scene in your mind and, in your own time, get ready to go home ... recharged, revitalized, renewed, content.

Being a tree
This one is good to do sitting in a chair with your feet flat on the floor. It is wonderful if you think you need 'grounding'.

Picture a rich brown, loamy forest floor in the late spring. Although there are many huge beech trees, oaks and sycamores the forest is not at all dark. There are wide, grassy glades where the sun streams in. What can you see? ... Primroses and wild cyclamen peeking out of the fertile carpet of last autumn's leaves? ... A shy doe and her fawn motionless in a clearing? ... A pair of Red Admiral butterflies drifting on the scented air? ... What can you hear? ... A woodpecker? ... A wood pigeon? ... A small furry animal rustling about in the undergrowth? ... What can you smell? ... Pine needles? ... Wood violets? ... Damp earth? ...

As you sit there, feel your feet begin to take root. Like a seedling, inch by inch, you feel your way down through the soil. Getting a firm grip on your existence, seeking your nourishment. Your roots extend and branch out, burrowing their way deep into the earth, ensuring that even in the driest summer you will be able to draw on the eternal well-springs of underground water. When you encounter buried rocks you feel your way around them, securing yourself, protecting yourself from wild winds, from fierce storms, from stags sharpening their antlers, from children climbing you. Nothing can dislodge you.

Your roots grow thicker and more plentiful. A mother fox makes her burrow amongst them and gives birth to her litter. Moles and earthworms inhabit this nether world. This is the deep, nourishing, darkness, the womb of the Earth where things grow and transform themselves, where waste is changed into compost. You are grounded, earthed, part of the planet. You hold the surface of the world together. You are in touch with the Earth's heartbeat.

While your roots grow down, your branches grow upwards, reaching for the sunlight, stretching towards the sky. Your sap is rising up through your trunk, coursing through your limbs, energizing your growth. Thousands of buds appear, tendrils of leaves unfurl. You are a source of beauty, of plenty, of shade and of fruit. Birds come and nest in your highest branches. All manner of insects go about their business. Bears rub their fur against your bark. You are a link between heaven and earth, between darkness and light, between the rocks and the stars. You will endure.

Gradually withdraw your roots and branches back into your human form. Allow a few minutes of quiet sitting before resuming normal life.

The terraces of flowers

This one is actually a guided walk through the colours associated with the chakras, starting with the lowest. It is an effective way to balance yourself.

You are in a room filled with whirring, clanking machinery. The incessant noise and distraction have made you tense. Constant demands are being made on you and it is impossible to get any peace and quiet. Suddenly you notice for the first time a small door on the far side of the room. When you open it you see it leads onto a little bridge. Walk through the door and close it behind you. The noise miraculously ceases. All you can hear is the delirious sound of larks high in the summer sky. You cross the bridge, go through a gate and find yourself in a garden at the base of a terraced hillside. You decide to walk to the top.

The level where you begin your walk is a field of red flowers. Red as far as you can see from east to west, from north to south. Millions of poppies, red tulips, red carnations, red roses, hibiscus, poinsettias and begonias. Breathe in their scent, feel the texture of their petals, allow the colour of red to saturate you as you walk.

As you reach the end of the red field there is another gate and a few steps up to the orange terrace. Orange flowers as far as the eye can see. Acres of orange dahlias, chrysanthemums and flaming gladioli. There are orange and tangerine trees, too, laden with fruit. Banks of nasturtiums and marigolds stretch into the distance. Breathe in the fresh smell of orange, feel the textures as you pass, allow the colour to permeate your skin.

As you reach the end of the orange terrace there is another gate and a few steps up to the yellow terrace. Before your eyes is a field of yellow daffodils. Walk slowly through the sea of yellow flowers. You can also see narcissi, jonquils, primroses, and yellow tulips. There are sunflowers, too, and mimosa trees and lemons. The colour of yellow fills your senses. Breathe it in, feel the textures as you pass. Yellow soaks into your skin with the sun shining down on you.

As you reach the end of the yellow terrace there is another gate and a few steps up to the green terrace. Smooth, velvety, emerald green grass inviting you to take off your shoes and walk barefoot. There are ferns in secret clumps and banks of moss. Mature trees, their branches thick with green summer leaves, fill your eyes and your heart. Greenness is everywhere and your senses drink it in. Your breath is coloured green and permeates your body.

As you reach the end of the green terrace there is another gate and a few steps up to the blue terrace. Here are bluebells in profusion, periwinkles, hyacinths and forget-me-nots. The sky is a very clear blue and you allow yourself to become flooded with the colour blue as you walk. Feel the texture of the flowers, breathe in their rich perfume.

As you reach the end of the blue terrace there is another gate and a few steps up to the indigo terrace. This is a carpet of pansies and violets. Fill your nostrils and your lungs with their heady scent. Dark velvet irises beckon you to touch their wonderful petals. Feel yourself saturated with the colour of indigo as you walk through.

As you reach the end of the indigo terrace there is another gate and a few steps up to the purple terrace. You are nearly at the top of the hill now and the overwhelming vista of purple lifts your spirits. Exquisite orchids are growing wild as far as the eye can see. Purple gloxinias and clumps of anemones. Big purple dahlias and bunches of wisteria on vines. Taste the purple, smell it, feel the texture of the petals as you pass, breathe in the colour purple and feel yourself soaring upwards.

Your feet are barely touching the ground as you come to a plateau on top of the hill. You can see a little building like a temple and you decide to go and sit there for a while before the homeward journey. Far off you see a person coming toward you. It is a wise and loving person ready to listen to you and answer any questions you might have. He or she has come especially to find you at the temple. You meet and embrace, feeling the welcome presence of this lovely person giving you joy and strength. It may be someone you have met before, someone you loved who died or a benevolent stranger, but you know you can tell the person anything, talk about any problem.

You stay together as long as you wish and just before parting, your wise being gives you a gift to take away with you and a promise to meet you here again whenever you need a friend. Wings have sprouted from your shoulders and you are able to soar above the fields of flowers all the way back to the room in which you are lying. Take some time to feel yourself truly back in the here and now in your body and to ponder the nature of the gift you received.

The search for truth
Piero Ferrucci in his book, *What We May Be*, retells an Oriental fable:

> One day the gods decided to create the Universe. They created the seas, the mountains, the flowers, and the clouds. Then they created human beings. At the end they created Truth.
>
> At this point, however, a problem arose: where should they hide Truth so that humans would not find it right away? They wanted to prolong the adventure of the search.
>
> 'Let's put Truth on top of the highest mountain,' said one of the gods. 'Certainly it will be hard to find it there.'
>
> 'Let's put in on the furthest star,' said another.
>
> 'Let's hide it in the darkest and deepest abyss.'
>
> 'Let's conceal it on the secret side of the moon.'
>
> At the end, the wisest and most ancient god said, 'No, we will hide Truth inside the very heart of human beings. In this way they will look for it all over the Universe, without being aware of having it inside themselves all the time.'

The meeting with our wise and kindly being at the temple on top of the hill is an encounter with the wisest part of ourselves, the all-knowing, non-judgemental higher self. It is an inner dialogue with the truth whereby ideas are clarified and fears dispelled. At times of crossroads or crisis this is a really useful technique to try. The gift you are given is a sort of talisman to help you keep faith with yourself. It is amazing what your mind will come up with.

Symbols and metaphors are two of the richest resources we have as human beings. We are tirelessly trying to find ways to make ourselves listen to the truth. We make metaphors in dreams all of the time, as if the subconscious mind is a library of cross-references constantly throwing up new images to clarify things, drawing our attention to what we need to know.

Sometimes, for example, you might meet an animal along your imaginary journeys or in your dreams. This is very special indeed. When you call up the power of an animal, you are asking to be drawn into harmony with the qualities of that creature's essence – courage, say, or patience, playfulness or diligence. You are acknowledging these potentials in yourself and asking for an ally. Animal medicine, the Native Americans call it.

Whenever guidance comes to you and in whatever form it appears, it is important to maintain an attitude of reverence and be willing to accept assistance. One of the most effective ways to restructure ourselves is by using our imagination. This is communication with an inner resource, contacting an inner guide. Trust that the wiser part of you has found a way to get in touch.

4
HOW TO DEVELOP YOUR OWN HEALING POWERS

There is a common misconception that to be able to heal you have to be an especially gifted person, but I don't agree. In fact I have become deeply committed to the idea that the ability to heal is no more or less miraculous than the ability to love, and that anyone can do it. All you need are a willing heart, the desire to learn and the courage to open yourself as a channel through which healing energy can flow.

Of course, like any natural attribute, some will have it in greater abundance than others. There will undoubtedly be genius healers and humble, workaday ones but that should not prevent anyone from developing their gifts to the best of their abilities. Even if you are not Pavarotti you can still enjoy singing. In fact singing is rather a good analogy. Most of us have lost confidence in our singing voices, having become intimidated by the high standard of professional recording artists. The truth is, though, that any baby would prefer a lullaby sung by its mother.

People usually approach healing from one of two different directions. Either they are facing a crisis themselves and are seeking help or they feel drawn to developing their own healing powers. Often the latter follows on naturally from the former. Many times I've heard people say, 'I discovered I had healing hands after I, myself, was healed of cancer.' Their frame of reference has been changed and expanded beyond all recognition, and they now have a different perspective on life and illness.

This is a very good time to think of developing your own latent potential. It is natural to want to give back something when you have been the recipient of healing. Like love, the best way to keep it is to give it away! Have you noticed how, generally in life, we don't always have the opportunity to repay gestures of kindness to the person we received them from but, instead, often get the chance to pass them on down the line? Like ripples on a pond, the circles spread outwards.

The common denominator of all healing methods is love and compassion or, as I heard someone describe it, 'Drawing the circle of our being larger and becoming more inclusive, more capable of loving.' Healing means giving others the kind of love and acceptance we ourselves would like to receive.

The great healer Harry Edwards once said, 'The desire to heal must come from the heart ... along with basic qualities of generosity of spirit and compassion there must be a willingness to be of service and a strong desire to take away pain and unhappiness.'

In addition to these basic qualities, the other requirement for a would-be healer is self-awareness, or at least the honesty to ask yourself a few uncomfortable questions about your motivation:

Why do I want to be a healer?

What am I hoping to get out of it?

Am I trying to create a smokescreen so as to avoid confronting my own needs?

Do I want to help others because I find it impossible to ask for help myself?

Would I really like someone to give me some healing instead?

Do I have rescue fantasies? A saviour complex? Is this an ego trip?

Like every other healer I know, I ask myself these questions repeatedly. There aren't any right answers – just monitor yourself. Part of a healer's sensitivity means being sensitive to your own needs and processes. We can't help anyone else until we have begun to put our own house in order.

Being needy doesn't bar you from healing (if it did there would be a lot of healers out of business!), but it does mean making sure you are getting those needs met. If not, it is the blind leading the blind and, to put it bluntly, you could be a menace. We must always remember that healing is given to help doctors and not to replace them.

Richard Moss, the American writer and healer, has said, 'As a healer your job is really to be a friend and supporter of healing, a travelling companion. But it is not *you* who does the healing. It is a big hazard to become seduced by the illusion of your power and wonderfulness. You need to keep in mind that the healing ability consists mainly of a gift for influencing, stimulating, encouraging and inspiring people to place one foot in front of another on their own healing path. And, of course, sometimes nothing you do will work.'

GETTING STARTED

First and foremost, it is the *quality* of healing relationships rather than any specific technique that is probably the foundation of healing, but so saying, there are two fundamental skills which form the basis of all healing work:

1. The ability to feel body-energy fields.
2. The ability to be a channel through which the fine vibrations of healing energy can travel. Thereafter, patience and practice are all you will need.

I am going to make a few suggestions as to various exercises that can be used to begin developing these skills, but I can't emphasize too strongly the importance of doing a course. There is no substitute for the group experience with its opportunities to learn and experiment with fellow seekers.

Many colleges and universities have courses that teach people how to develop their healing powers. Nurses frequently use this type of therapy to alleviate pain. In fact, it is so important to their practice that courses in therapeutic touch are included in many nursing school curricula and continuing education programs. It is not restricted to health care practitioners, however – anyone can learn the technique.

In the meantime, to get you started . . .

Experiencing the energy
Nearly all these exercises require a partner so try to get a friend or family member to come and play.

First rub your hands vigorously together for a few

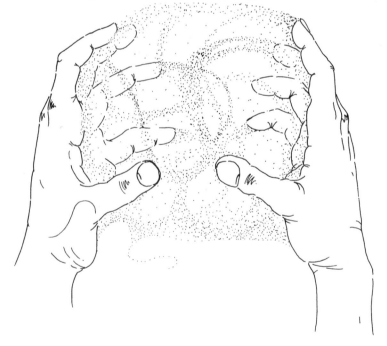

Fig. 5 Beginning to feel the energy

seconds until you feel a sort of static electrical charge, the kind that picks up scraps of tissue paper with a comb after you've run it through your hair. Now hold them about an inch apart. Can you feel a warmth, a tingling or something like a force field?

We are not always aware of the energy field around our bodies and yet we feel uncomfortable if someone breaches our personal space without being invited. It is this auric space that we are trying consciously to discern. Experiment with moving your hands nearer and further apart to see if the strength of the energy varies. Try shaping it into a ball and playing with the size and shape of it, expanding and contracting it (see Fig. 5). Try holding your hands near your face.

Once you have begun to feel your own energy, have your partner put one hand between your two, not quite touching, and see what that feels like. Again experiment with distances. Reverse roles and compare notes. Take plenty of time over this. Sometimes, even if you don't feel that you are being very successful at 'calling up' the energy, your partner will be able to feel a warmth or gentle radiation coming from your hands.

The more feedback you can get, the better. Don't be discouraged. Everybody feels a bit tentative to begin with. You are in an area where no one can validate you. You have to learn to trust your feelings. If someone else feels it at the same time, that's a fact. You need facts as well as happenings!

Feeling the flow

I once saw a remarkable demonstration of this at a healing workshop. The teacher stood up and extended one arm out to the side. He invited the strongest man in the group to come forward and force his arm back down again. Of course it was easily done. The arm in that position has very little strength. Then the teacher told us that he was going to visualize his arm as a high pressure fire hose gushing out water at enormous velocity. This time the strongest man couldn't budge it (see Fig. 6).

Fig. 6 Getting in touch with the limitless source

This is the principle that martial arts practitioners use to break a stack of roof tiles – harnessing the mental energy and directing it. Like all energy, it is neutral. The use to which it is put depends on who is using it.

Try the firehouse trick yourself, visualzing the water pouring in through the crown of your head and out through your arm, and see how much the mental component augments your physical strength. If you can also picture the energy as coming from a limitless source – divine or cosmic, whichever you are comfortable with – you are on your way.

Getting into the healing mode is an act of intention so it is helpful to begin with a short meditative preparation.

Sit facing your partner as near as feels comfortable, with your back supported and your hands cupped one in the other, palms up, at the level of your solar plexus. Centre yourselves by closing your eyes and taking five or six deep breaths. Count backwards from 10, slowing yourself down, becoming still, gathering yourself into your heart. As one of the lecturers on as NFSH course once put it, 'We are trying to link ourselves with the inexhaustible motive power that spins the universe.' The links are our imagination and our breathing. More than a mere inhalation of chemicals, *prana*, the Sanskrit word for breath, also means 'soul'. It is airborne magic, the essence that effects consciousness.

There is a beautiful visualization that you can do at this point calles the energy spiral. It links all your major chakras, knees, elbows, feet and hands. It encompasses the auric space around you and connects you to the transpersonal point above your head. It is a wonderful way of spinning a cocoon of energy around yourself and making yourself ready for healing (see Fig. 7).

Think of yourself in the position of Leonardo's man with outstretched arms and legs, enclosed in a circle. Beginning in your heart chakra, draw a mental spiral that goes down to your solar plexus, up to your mid chest, down to your abdomen, up to your throat, down to your base chakra, up to your brow, down to your knees and up to your crown passing through your elbows, down through your feet and up to the transpersonal point passing through your hands.

Now reach out and lightly rest your hands, palm to palm, with your partner's and imagine yourselves both

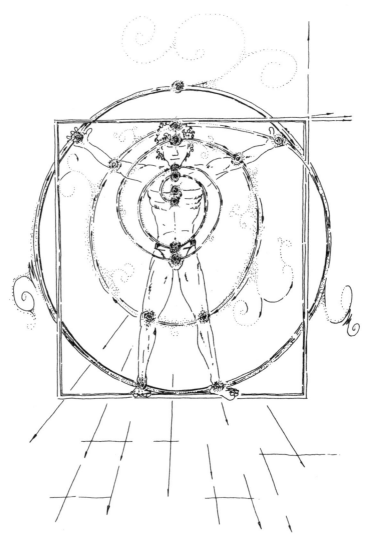

Fig. 7 The opening energy spiral

enclosed within a protective capsule of white light. This is a symbolic way of shielding yourselves from any psychic harm and of keeping all distractions at bay.

In this position, with your eyes closed, see if you can

send a beam of pure heart energy diagonally across to your partner's heart (see Fig. 8). The emphasis is on giving. Think of it as a loving benediction. There is no greater gift one can offer than the energy of unconditional presence.

This is a very fine, loving energy and the quality of it is much more important than the intensity. It is neither sexual nor emotional but heart energy – entirely pure and beautiful. Keep your ego out of the way. It is not *your* energy, it is *ours*. Universal, cosmic, unconditional, divine – it is simply passing through. Just feel your crown opening and let it in.

Keep up this transmission for about 10 minutes and then gradually begin to withdraw the energy. Feel the crown close down again like a camera lens. Slowly disconnect your hands, open your eyes and spend some time discussing the sensations both of giving and receiving.

In the second exercise, start in the same way and after a few minutes bring some of the heart energy up to your throat chakra and down your arms into your hands. This is an exercise I learned from the wonderful American teacher, Brugh Joy. He suggests that each person imagines a fusion of energy flow like a ball of light at the point where the two pairs of hands join. Keep the heart energy radiating at the same time. In addition, while your heart is so open, see if you can pick up an image or intuition about your partner. Although you may know the person well, a new insight could possibly present itself to you, helping you to view them in an even more compassionate way.

Again, after about 10–15 minutes, withdraw the energy back into your heart, disconnect hands, open your eyes and share, with your partner, what you felt or didn't feel.

The third exercise is designed to demonstrate how different it feels when only one partner is transmitting. Begin in the same way – centering and shielding – deciding in advance who is going to be A and B. This time, after a couple of minutes, partner A stops transmitting and just enters into a receptive state of consciousness while partner B continues actively to send energy through

Fig. 8 Sending a beam of pure heart energy

the heart and through the hands. After about five minutes, reverse roles then for the last five minutes, both resume transmitting again.

Take some time, after withdrawing, disconnecting and opening your eyes, to share your experiences with each other.

You are beginning to play with the energy now. Try this one:

The point is to resist your partner's flow as hard as possible while they try any devious means to sneak the energy in. The first time I ever tried this I was astonished by how exhausting it is to resist. My whole arm ached as if I were trying to hold back a truck with no brakes on a downhill slope. When I finally allowed the flow again it rushed through like pumping blood when a tourniquet is removed. It made me aware of how much energy we expend in keeping other people out. Being able to surrender in an atmosphere of trust is such a welcome relief and learning to trust is as important as learning to give.

The following exercise is a beautiful one to do:

Partner A curls up in a ball allowing herself to feel isolated, self-protective, rejected, misunderstood. Partner B, with infinite sensitivity and tenderness, focusses all his attention on directing healing heart-energy to where it is most needed. At first it may not be desirable to make contact with the body. If your partner is radiating a touch-me-not force field, you don't want to barge through it or you will create a very threatening atmosphere. Trust your intuition as to what will help her to feel safe. Often, mentally directing the energy first is a good way to start, followed by a gentle laying of hands on the spine or feet. There are no precise rules. The idea is to develop your awareness and to fine-tune your sensitivity (see Fig. 9).

As partner A begins to feel the effect she will slowly uncurl and relax. Her breathing will deepen and you will feel the tension gradually loosen as she lowers her defences in response to your loving care. This exercise takes as long as it takes but usually within half an hour your prickly hedgehog will have turned into a purring cat. After a short break, perhaps for a cup of tea, reverse roles.

Finally, a lovely energy balancing exercise. This is the one I use most frequently when I want to give a general healing.

Have your partner lie on the floor with a pillow under her head and knees if lying on her back, under head and hips if lying face down. You begin by doing a scan of her energy field. Kneeling to one side and working about five inches above the body, run your hands in a single smooth, continuous motion from the top of the head down to the feet. What you are trying to assess is whether there are any areas of imbalance or congestion in the energy field. These can be felt as differences in temperature or patches of disturbance or deficit.

Once again we are into the inadequacy of everyday language to describe these subtle changes. You are trying to attune yourself to the rhythm of your partner. One of the points that is always emphasized in therapeutic touch classes is *not* to focus on any illness or problem but to acknowledge and salute the true individuality or essence of the other person – which is much deeper and more inclusive than the illness. The point of the healing is to try to strengthen the individual's inner tendency toward order and wholeness.

Remember, this is not a diagnosis but a technique for picking up as much information about the state of your friend's energy as you can. You are opening the channels to your own inner knowing. Don't worry if you can't feel much to begin with. You will certainly become more confident at being able to discern these subtle clues with practice. It's also a method of concentration, enabling you to enter the state of mind needed to be of service. This is where intention and sincerity of purpose come in.

Now, continuing to work a few inches above the body, if that feels right to you, or laying hands on directly, seat yourself cross-legged on the right hand side of your friend and gently place your hands over the depleted area. Just stay quietly in that position for a few minutes channelling

Fig. 9 Fine-tuning your sensitivity

energy. If you also know that your friend has been experiencing any pain or discomfort, devote some time to removing it.

This is done by visualizing 'drawing off' the pain into your hands rather in the manner of a magnet or a poultice and allowing it to discharge harmlessly through you into the ground. Alternatively you can gently shake your hands as if they were wet. (Gently is the operative word. It is very off-putting when healers make a big theatrical production out of flinging the invisible energy from them as if it were toxic radioactive waste!)

Finally balance up the whole body by starting at the feet and working your way up through the joints and chakras by lightly holding each point for a few minutes. It's a way of filling a person up when they are depleted and can often be used as a sort of first aid. I find that I like to take a moment or two to attune myself to my 'patient' and to sense, with the aid of visualization, the energy running through my own body like a shimmering current of sparkling particles. Then as I lay my hands on my partner I silently ask permission of her higher self for my intervention and feel guided both to channel in and draw off energy, whichever seems appropriate.

Once you have begun a healing session you are in a sacred space. There is something hallowed about the transaction where anything might happen and nothing is impossible. I often think of the words of one of my teachers, Rosalyn Bruyere, the gifted American healer: 'Be delicate with your movements,' she said. 'Be reverent with the body. And remember, the patient is the best archaeologist on their dig! Ask them what they are feeling. Pay attention, listen for cues. Don't run your own trip.'

At best it can have a remarkable effect and be a point of transformation. At the very least it will provide a general tonic that recharges the body's auto-immune system.

At the end of the session, your partner will be 'well away' as we say, in a very relaxed state, possibly even asleep. Signal that you have finished by a light squeeze of the hand or brushing of the cheek and bring her gently

Fig. 10 Closing energy spiral

back to the here and now. Suggest she wriggles her fingers and toes, has a little stretch, and gradually, in her own time, opens her eyes.

Do a closing spiral, which is the reverse of the opening one, bringing the energy back into your own heart (see Fig. 10).

Remain close, sharing the feelings and intuitions from the experience for a few moments, then close down your crown, dissolve the protective shield and you're both ready for the outside world.

5
THE USE OF THE SENSES

If we can accept the concept of the body being composed of interdependent fields of energy, it begins to make sense to assume that destructive patterns which have manifested as illness can be influenced by vibrational frequencies.

Physics and biology are beginning to uncover the answer to mysteries which until recently have rather been the preserve of poets and mystics. We now understand that matter and energy are two different manifestations of the same primary energy of which everything in the universe is composed. The slower the vibrationary rate the denser the matter – rocks, trees, bone, flesh; the faster the vibrationary rate the more subtle the energy – sound, light, colour.

In order to make changes in the patterns we have created we can administer very high-frequency, subtle energy and this is what is known as vibrational medicine. All the vibrational remedies offer us a set of tools to help mobilize the body's self-healing abilities.

TOUCH

First and foremost of these tools is touch, and we have seen how the theraputic use of loving touch combined with relaxation, the conscious use of breathing and visualization can greatly aid a person's potential for change.

It is the simplest and most natural thing that one human being can do for another, complete in itself and often all that is needed. However, the addition of one or more of the complementary vibrational remedies, bringing in the other senses, gives healing another dimension.

Before I had ever read about these things I instinctively felt that subtle energies were all around me if only I knew how to use them. Once when my husband had been troubled by a painful rheumatic knee for weeks and the specialist had told him, 'What do you expect at your age? Come back when it gets worse and I'll put you on steroids,' I decided to follow my intuition. I gave him some gentle laying-on-of-hands in a quiet candlelit room followed by a massage with a crystal. It seemed to me that the pitch of a cello would be a comforting resonance to aim at his knees so I put on a recording of Dvorak's Cello concerto while all this was going on.

The knee was greatly improved the next morning and the pain was completely gone in two or three days.

CRYSTALS

That was my first experience of one of the many uses to which crystals can be put. Healer Soozi Holbeche who uses crystals all the time reminds us in her book, *The Power of Gems and Crystals*:

> The word disaster literally means (in Latin) 'separation from the stars' ... separation from light and joy, from love and laughter. We are separate from our own perfection, our own divinity.
>
> Quartz crystals can help us make that quantum leap to the stars. They are like crystallized light – starlight. They are the most evolved stone of the mineral kingdom.

We use crystals daily, without thinking, in all kinds of ways – in communication technology, information storage, liquid crystal displays, solar power, and laser applications in medicine and industry to name but a few. Many ancient civilizations also understood the remarkable properties of crystals and we should be wary of dismissing their technology as primitive. An aboriginal medicine man I stayed with in Australia had some small quartz crystals among the power objects he carried in a little bag around his neck.

In *Vibrational Medicine,* Dr Richard Gerber quotes from an interview with Marcel Vogel, a senior scientist with IBM for twenty-seven years who had this to say about crystals and their use in healing:

> The crystal is a neutral object whose inner structure exhibits a state of perfection and balance. When it's cut to the proper form and when the human mind enters into a relationship with its structural perfection, *the crystal emits a vibration* which extends and amplifies the powers of the user's mind. Like a laser it radiates energy in a coherent, highly concentrated form, and this energy may be transmitted into objects or people at will ... its higher purpose ... is in the service of humanity for the removal of pain and suffering. (my italics)

I have always known that a crystal can augment and focus any natural energies that I may have, acting like a laser in directing them. It seems to organize the energy in some way. I now use crystals regularly for rebalancing and cleansing the chakras, for diminishing pain, for amplifying the healing power of touch directly onto a problem area, such as a broken bone or a backache, and for sending absent healing to a person some distance away.

Choosing a crystal

The whole business of choosing a crystal is a curious process. I have found, and many friends have echoed my findings, that if I buy myself a crystal in a shop it will only be a matter of time before I will experience a sudden overwhelming urge to give it away to someone. However, if I find a crystal in a cave or on a beach or, better still, if someone gives me one as an unexpected gift, then it stays with me forever. In other words, *they* choose *you.*

This may seem a bit fanciful and I agree that, as yet, there isn't really an adequate explanation, but a bit of whimsy never did any harm and there may well be a perfectly logical reason – sympathetic resonance perhaps? – which will become clear when we know more. Take your time when choosing a crystal to buy. Stand in front of the showcase for a while and wait until one particular crystal catches your eye and draws your attention. Hold it in your hand and feel its texture and weight. It will either feel right or it won't. Trust your intuition.

I have crystals all over my house and I always carry one in my handbag. I take them with me when I give lectures and workshops, I wear them around my neck for healing and protection. At the very least they are beautiful and companionable, and there seems quite a lot of evidence that they can help us in our transformational endeavours. It is believed that quartz crystals are natural purifiers of energy because they absorb negative energies and transmit positive beneficial ones.

The next step is to cleanse your crystal. The latest hypothesis is that crystals store energy in a 'memory' in much the same way that a computer floppy disc does. By clearing it of old energy programming you will put it into fresh, receptive state, ready to be charged with a new energetic thought form or function. The best way is to leave it soaking overnight in a bowl of water with sea salt or in a bowl of spring water with a few drops of Pennyroyal flower essence.

Now your crystals can be used either for meditation or for healing. (It is advisable to keep separate crystals for different functions.) A small crystal pendant can also be used to augment inner knowing by dowsing.

Another way to utilize crystal energy is to drink *gem elixirs*. These are made by leaving a crystal in water and charging it in direct sunlight. The subtle vibrations are transferred to the water in much the same way as happens with homeopathic remedies, and the water is imprinted with the particular energy and healing qualities of the crystal.

To enhance meditation and visualization, hold a crystal in your left hand. The reason for this is because the right

Fig. 11 The hemispheres of the brain

hemisphere of the brain (which is connected to the left side of the body) is the one associated with the more intuitive, imaginative faculties of the mind. It is thought that the crystal can have a resonant effect on the crystal-line structures of the pineal gland which may help to unlock the hidden potential of the right hemisphere and give better access to the symbolic and metaphoric capabilities of the mind (see Fig. 11).

For a quick re-energizing and rejuvenation of your body, hold a crystal in each hand, the crystal in your left hand pointing towards your wrist, the one in your right hand pointing away from you. Try this for five or ten minutes when you are tired and you will be amazed at the difference it makes.

A slightly more advanced meditation technique is to

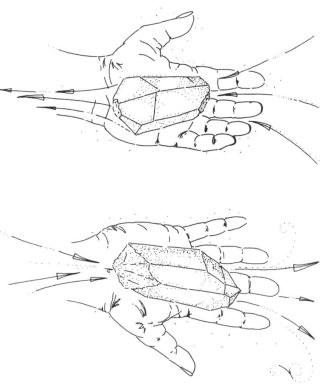

Fig. 12 Re-energizing yourself with crystals

Fig. 13 An energy grid

create an energy grid by placing a crystal in each of the
four corners of the room where you are going to sit or by
placing them in the pattern of a six-pointed star
(imagining the lines connecting up to form a geometric
pattern). Then if you sit in the centre of the grid holding a
focal crystal you become part of the network of energy (see
Fig. 13).

Dowsing is not just the paranormal way to discover
water beneath the ground, although it has been used this
way very successfully for thousands of years. Dowsing
with a small crystal pendulum on a string or chain can be
used as a way to get yes or no answers to questions. By
holding your crystal suspended and asking it which way
it swings to signify yes and which way it swings to signify
no you can establish a dialogue with the wisest part of
yourself (see Fig. 14). Of course the crystal cannot tell you
things in itself but like any method of divination (the tarot,
the *I Ching*, runes), it augments and helps bring to con-
sciouness things that you already know. Then when you
ask important questions about the choices you have to
make in your life it becomes easier to clarify your thoughts.

To use crystals for healing, choose one that you can hold
comfortably with the base pressed firmly against the palm
of your hand, point down. To take pain out of the body,

Fig. 14 Dowsing with a crystal

hold the crystal in your left hand (the receptive hand) and circle it in an anti-clockwise direction about 4 or 5 inches above the trouble spot for as long as seems appropriate. To direct healing into the body, hold the crystal in the right hand (the transmitting hand) and circle it in a clockwise direction. Always give your very best attention to this work and finish by visualizing light and healing being magnified by the crystal, pouring through you and into the 'patient'. Vogel again: 'The crystal ... *when used with love, makes the energies of the mind coherent.* It brings these energies into a pattern exactly fitting the life energies of the person seeking to be healed and then amplifies them for healing.' (my italics again)

Crystal healing can be done as a general tonic to balance the chakras as well as for a specific ailment. One good way is to lie down and place a crystal on your base chakra with the pointed end towards your head. Visualize a little meter over the site of the chakra with the needle pointing haphazardly every which way and keep the crystal in position until it settles at 90 degrees. Work your way up each chakra in turn until you have visualized them all perfectly balanced (see Fig. 15).

Quartz crystals, because they are the most all-embracing, can be used on all the chakras very successfully, but you could also select gemstones that relate to the associated colour of individual chakras and choose gem elixirs in the same way if you are trying to treat a specific deficiency. Gemstones have been prized since antiquity not only for their beauty but for the way their vibrationary forces correlate with the human body.

Gemstones and chakras
1. Root or base chakra – red stones, e.g. rubies, bloodstone, garnets. These can stimulate energy, vitality and the regeneration of cells, blood and tissue.

2. Abdominal or sacral chakra – orange stones, e.g. fire opals, topaz, wulfenite, amber. These are good for the digestive system and for balancing and integrating the emotions.

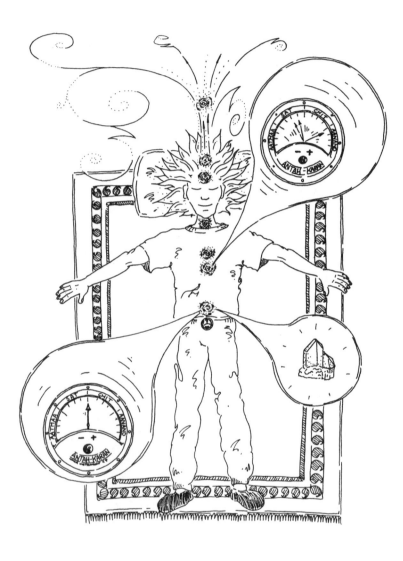

Fig. 15 A visualisation for balancing the chakras

3. Solar plexus chakra – yellow stones, e.g. citrine, very pale topaz, yellow sapphire, yellow diamond or zircon. These are joyful, cheerful stones which help us to develop the intellect and our powers of discernment. Good for clarity of mind.

4. Heart chakra – green stones, e.g. emeralds, jade, peridot, green garnets. These are soothing and calming. Very useful in treating fear, and timidity. Helpful in opening the heart to love.

5. Throat chakra – blue stones, e.g. sapphires, turquoise, aquamarine, lapis lazuli. These are associated with wisdom, truth and communication. Helpful for speaking out and letting your voice be heard.

6. Brow chakra – indigo stones, e.g. alexandrite, tourmaline, dark sapphires, bluish amethysts. These stones help to activate the third eye, the faculty of inner vision. Helpful for developing psychic or extra-sensory perception and intuition.

7. Crown chakra – purple stones, e.g. amethysts, rose quartz, sodalite, fluorite. Wonderful stones to aid meditation. Helpful for creativity, inspiration and developing spiritual awareness.

A further use for the marvellous amplifying power of crystals is in sending absent healing to someone whom you can't be physically near. This is really another example of energetic resonance. By holding a crystal and 'programming it' with a healing thought form you can thereby magnify the effect of sending the healing over any distance. The clearer the thought or image you can hold in your mind, the more effective the transmission will be. Time and space are no barrier and you can be anywhere with the speed of your thoughts. You could also charge the crystal with energy and give it or send it to the patient to hold.

Do experiment with crystals. I think they are one of the natural world's most miraculous and most underrated gifts to mankind.

THE SENSE OF SMELL

Our sense of smell has become rather neglected. Apart from warning us if the house is on fire or there is a gas leak, it is not such a vital part of our survival mechanisms as it was in ancient times and yet it is more powerful than we think. The quickest way to evoke a memory, trigger an emotion or a sexual response is via the olfactory receptors. They send the odours to our emotional centre in the brain called the limbic system. This extremely active system is connected to other vital parts of the brain involved in controlling heart rate, blood pressure, breathing, memory and reaction to stress. A faint trail of a perfume you thought you'd forgotten, the scent of a gardenia or a freshly powdered baby, a whiff of school dinners and you are transported *instantly* back in time to the place where you last experienced that smell.

Aromatherapy is the name given to a therapeutic treatment combining massage and essential oils. It is one of the loveliest forms of healing you can have – relaxing, nurturing, stimulating. As well as its usefulness in restoring balance, enhancing well-being and being used to treat a variety of conditions, it is also a valuable preventive therapy.

To become a qualified aromatherapist requires a rigorous training in anatomy, physiology, massage and a knowledge of the healing properties of over fifty essential oils. However, anyone can buy the little bottles of the oils and use them at home. Essential oils are distilled from flowers, seeds, grasses, bark, leaves, roots, stalks, resins and fruits. They are the concentrated life-force of the plant and, apart from smelling wonderful, each one has specific therapeutic qualities. It's a good idea to buy a book or do an introductory course in aromatherapy in order to learn which oils are good for what, but you can also trust your intuition and just go for what you like. It is important to buy only pure and natural essences. These are expensive, but the synthetic ones simply do not do the job.

How to use them

Essential oils are not really oily at all. They are, in fact, volatile, magical essences that evaporate quickly if left exposed to the air. A few drops can be added to a good quality carrier oil such as almond, soya or sunflower oil for a delicious massage. Actually, I always make up a 50 ml bottle of my own favourite basic massage oil mixture and keep it ready. Here is the recipe:

> 1 tsp. hazelnut or avocado oil (this is quite expensive but has very good penetrative powers)

> 1 tsp. wheatgerm oil (this is good for dry skin and also improves the keeping quality of the basic oil)

> Fill up the bottle with rapeseed oil (this is a fine, clear, odourless oil readily available from any supermarket and also, fortunately, one of the cheapest). Then just before giving a massage, pour some into a small saucer and add a few drops of one or more essential oils.

If you want to begin a little collection of essential oils, I would like to suggest 12 of my favourites (with a warning that you will get hooked on this and always want to be adding more!). They vary in price because of their relative rarity and the complexity of the procedure required to extract them. Be sure to purchase them from a reputable supplier.

Lavender: Refreshing and relaxing. Good for healing headaches and burns.
Bergamot: Uplifting and refreshing.
Marjoram: Fortifying, helps to disperse bruises.
(These three together, 6 drops of each, makes a good warming and relaxing blend.)
Myrrh: Astringent, antiseptic, anti-inflammatory.

Neroli (orange blossom): Sedative, anti-depressant – very good for anxiety, fear or shock.

Sandalwood: Good for male troubles (e.g. impotence), dry skin, relieves itching.

Rosemary: Good for muscular or rheumatic pain, nerve stimulant, invigorating, refreshing.

Rose: Aphrodisiac, antiseptic, good for women's troubles, stress and nervous tension.

Geranium: Wonderful healing agent for wounds, burns and fractures.

Peppermint: Cooling, analgesic, good for skin irritation and digestive disorders.

Juniper: Tonic for the nervous system, digestive stimulant.

Tea Tree: Miraculous Australian oil known to the Aborigines for thousands of years, excellent antiseptic.

Experiment with your own blends. You will be astonished how these beautiful essences can uplift the spirits, reduce stress and tension, and relax frayed nerves and tight muscles.

One idea for using them is to put a few drops in a vaporizer. This will fill a room with a delicious fragrance and help to create a healing mood. For a healing session, probably the best way to use them is to put a little water in the top part with a few drops of the essence of your choice and then light the candle in the bottom part. As the water warms, the oil will gradually evaporate into the air (see Fig. 16). You can also put a few drops on a light bulb before switching it on.

MUSIC AND SOUND

'In the beginning was the word and the word was God.' It is a very ancient idea that the entire universe was created by sound. Richard Gerber, in *Vibrational Medicine*, writes, 'As scientists begin to understand the relationship between the vibrational patterns of sound and the structure of matter, they will tap into a whole new universe of

Fig. 16 Using a vaporizer with essential oils

ideas and applications of energy for healing and technology.'

The Australian Aborigines believe that in 'the dreamtime', which is part of their creation myth, the entire universe was sung into being.

The application of ultrasound techniques which utilize the vibrational frequencies of sound waves to affect the healing of sprains, fractures and other injuries has become standard practice in Western medicine but, apart from that, sound is a rather under-exploited resource. Yet chants and mantras have been used for thousands of years to avert danger, to lift the spirits, to heal the earth.

Once again, we seem to have lost touch with what is still part of more primary cultures – the unself-conscious freedom to dance and sing and chant. Everyone in an African village, from newborn babies to ancient crones, participates in dancing and music-making. It provides not only an ecstatic release in the original sense of the word – to get outside of the self – but also a perfect opportunity to 'be in tune' with you rcommunity. Every culture has its sacred songs, its folk songs, its profane songs and its traditions of chanting. To a certain extent, singing in church used to provide this communal outlet at least once a week, but even that is now the exception rather than the rule. All we have left is the annual Christmas carol ritual.

The very words we use to describe healing as a state of harmony and fine tuning are metaphors taken from music, and the spontaneous expression of feelings through music, dance and sound is a great aid to the healing process. I can't be the only person who furtively waits until everyone else is out of the house before putting on some wild music and dancing myself silly. I sing at the top of my voice when I'm alone in the car and I sometimes shout or wail or howl when I'm walking along a cliff top or a deserted beach and know I will not be heard. It is the best way I know to release anger, to express joy, to celebrate life, to give thanks, to let out frustrations, to voice grief.

Current thinking in the field of holistic healing is recognizing the need to explore sound and dance which, of course, are yet further ways of pressing vibrational frequencies into service. At Harperbury Hospital they are pioneering the use of *vibracoustic therapy* for people with mental and physical disabilities. Patients relax in a specially constructed chair which has a number of speakers built into it. Low-frequency sound waves combined with music from the speakers move through the body, soothing the mind and producing a profound sense of calm. Research has shown good results with a wide range of conditions from asthma to multiple sclerosis. Blood pressure is reduced along with anxiety and stress. Chronic illness due to neuroses is also reduced and spasticity and tightness in muscles alleviated. When you chant or hum, your whole body *becomes* the musical instrument and resonates with the pitch of the tone. When you dance you are literally planting your feet in the earth. It is a wonderful way to ground yourself.

In the book of Samuel in the Bible there is a description of how, when an evil spirit possessed Saul, the young David played to him on a harp. Saul was refreshed, 'and the evil spirit departed from him.' Also, in Homer's *Odyssey*, when Ulysses was wounded during the seige of Troy, Autolycus sang a magic melody to staunch the flow of blood. The vibrational patterns of sound may well hold the key to understanding the way that matter manifests and organizes itself in the universe, and the use of various frequencies of sound with crystals for healing is just the beginning of a whole new approach to healing (or, perhaps, the rediscovery of an old one).

A humming vibration has the capacity to cause a deep-level relaxation and rebalancing. Just as with listening to music, humming enables you to let go more and more deeply. Mentally projecting a hum into a particular part of the body has the effect of relaxing that part while at the same time facilitating a connecting up of the chakras. For example, humming into the lower abdomen while placing a hand over the 5th or sacral chakra has the effect of immediately reducing anxiety (see Fig. 17). You can do this for yourself on a plane, before taking a driving test, during childbirth or at the dentist's. You will notice an instant calming and relaxing effect. If it is inappropriate to hum out loud you can even imagine it and it still works!

The other interesting thing to notice is that you will automatically choose the right pitch to hum. The range of certain instruments corresponds to particular chakras or areas of the body and it is this, along with purely subjective instinct, which guides me to the choices I make for

Fig. 17 Use humming to reduce anxiety

healing music – hence Dvorak's Cello concerto for the knees! Bach's Double violin concerto goes straight to the heart. Australian didgeridoo music enters my body via the soles of my feet, the music of the Russian Orthodox Church centres itself right in the solar plexus, the pure tones of a boy soprano lift me into the stratosphere, Mozart's Clarinet concerto fills my head, African drumming or the heavy pulse of a bass guitar activates my body heat and sexual drive.

There are many therapeutic ways of using sound, chanting, movement, dance and music for tapping into very deep emotions. Of the three techniques in particular that I use for healing, one is the more passive listening meditation, the second is the active humming meditation (with or without crystals) and the third is the even more active movement or dance meditation. Do try them, they are great inhibition busters.

Listening meditation

For the listening meditation choose a piece of music (I include a short list of some of my favourites at the end of this chapter) and lie down in a warm, comfortable room with a couple of cushions under your knees so as not to put any strain on your lower back. Close your eyes, begin to breathe deeply and count yourself slowly backward from 10.

Piero Ferrucci, in his book *What We May Be* writes:

We do not need research to know that the magnificence of a cathedral's rose window, the design of Celtic manuscripts, a flower in full bloom or the perfect geometry of a Greek temple does not leave us unaffected. And the moment we let ourselves be touched by beauty, that part of us which has been badly bruised or even shattered by the events of life may begin to be revitalized. At that moment a true victory takes place – a victory over discouragement ... for the moment we fully appreciate beauty we become more than we were. We live a moment of pure psychological health. We effortlessly build a stronghold against the negative pressures that life invariably brings.

There is a self-transcending quality to music. It can infiltrate our defences like nothing else. It seems to awaken a remembrance of bliss and wholeness, enticing us out of the world of ordinary cares and concerns into a greater sphere of harmony and aliveness.

Maybe the effect of the music is actually to harmonize

the body's energy fields and with the stimulation of the music, body areas that are not ordinarily sensed may emerge into the awareness. You may become conscious of blockages in your own energy flow. It is possible to relieve any discomfort by imagining a flow of energy or a wash of colour through the congested area.

I once tried this when I had a backache. I had been overdoing it and knew I needed to relax. I was lying down and playing myself a recording of Fauré's *Requiem* when I had a strong image of my kidneys. I don't often give them much consideration, I have to confess, but it became quite clear that the backache was to do with the kidneys. I sent them some blue colour imagery, massaged them with a crystal and made myself drink several litres of spring water over the course of the next few days and all was well. It was the music which seemed to put me in touch with my body.

Often I will do a laying-on-of-hands healing while a person is in this meditative state, listening to a piece of music of her choice. Later the same piece of music played at home will evoke the body sensations during the energy transfer, enabling the person to stimulate her own chakra system and carry on with her own healing. Always remember that the most important thing a healer can accomplish is to do himself out of a job.

Beethoven once said that 'music is a higher revelation than all wisdom and philosophy'. The beauty of it discloses to us what is beyond thought. Our personal world has to be nourished from outside its boundaries, because, if isolated it cannot find in itself the resources to survive and the tools to solve its own difficulties.

Let yourself dissolve and surrender into the music. Without doing anything in particular it is a way of going through a door into a richer landscape (see Fig. 18). Breathe it in. Feel the music travelling under the surface of your skin and permeating your whole being as you did with the colour meditation. It is a way of allowing the life-force that courses through your body to make its own adjustments. Surrendering is not passive. It is a courageous leap into the unknown. It literally means rendering to a higher source. Trust whatever it brings and don't try to control it. If you find it hard to trust, this is a good place to start. Listening to music is an act of pure receiving.

When the piece of music has finished, allow yourself a bit of time to come back to earth. Don't drive your car for half an hour or so as you might feel a little 'spacey'.

Humming meditation

This one is better to do in a comfortable sitting position. If you feel self-conscious lock the door or go somewhere where you won't be disturbed or overheard. (In a nice hot bath is quite a good place – the water amplifies the sound vibrations. I sometimes hum underwater at the swimming pool.) Just begin breathing and with the out breath allow a humming vibration to come naturally. Experiment with different tones and feel where they resonate in your body. Breathe in and out, lengthening the out breath each time and humming until you run out of air.

Try placing your hands over a chakra or any area where there is pain or injury as you hum and as you breathe out. Sense your breath flowing out through your hands. You can literally 're-tune' yourself in this way. Don't try to make anything happen – just be open and receptive. You can also hum your sound and visualize a particular chakra as an opening window through which the sound is projected. You will probably find that wherever you project your hum, that part of the body will soften. It is no coincidence that mothers often hum lullabies to their babies. It is a vibration that makes us feel safe, connected and relaxed.

Humming, combined with foot massage, has been tried quite successfully with autistic children. They are often very musical and respond well to this approach. My mother, who did a lot of pioneering work with autistic children in the 1950s, first tried this with a little boy who was very disturbed and spent all day rocking and rhythmically banging his head. As soon as she sat near him and hummed the theme from Beethoven's Symphony no. 9

he became still. She held his little feet firmly, massaging the spinal reflex along the inside of each foot and repeatedly hummed the same theme over and over again. After about ten minutes he started humming too, which was very thrilling as he had not communicated before in any other way except for high-pitched shrieks. Thereafter, whenever he wanted her attention, he would sit himself in front of her, take her hands and place them on either side of his face and hum the theme from Beethoven's 9th.

When I use humming during a healing session I just add my own humming energy to the patient's as I place my hands over her body. The two sound invariably create a harmonious combination and if you have ever been in a group meditation with chanting or humming you will know that there is always a lovely harmony created as people attune themselves to each other.

This is a very interesting field of growing interest to scientists. It has already been suggested that neural networks in the brain may be responsive to harmonic principles in general and that human beings have an inbuilt urge to maintain a state of aesthetic order and harmonic balance essential to physical, mental and spiritual health.

DANCE OR MOVEMENT MEDITATION

The recent growth of popularity in sacred dance, whether it be Egyptian temple dancing or Bulgarian circle dancing, indicates how many of us would like to revive this ancient expressive and pleasurable tradition. Well there's nothing to stop you exploring this important form of meditation. All you need is a place where you are free to move and to make a noise. It's lovely to be outdoors if you can but the privacy of your own home will do fine.

Choose a piece of music to suit your mood, anything from Stravinsky to the Rolling Stones, from Respighi to reggae, and begin just to bounce up and down to the beat. You are not trying to choreograph a performance piece but to *become* the music. Let yourseif move freely, loosely,

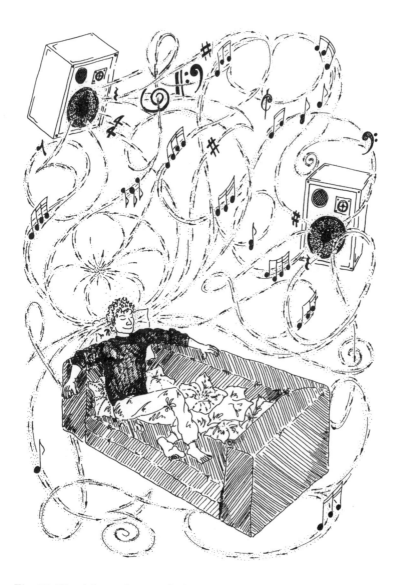

Fig. 18 Dissolving and surrendering into the music

unself-consciously. Don't be concerned about looking silly; just allow your body to respond to the quality of the music. After you've warmed up, put a bit more energy into it. Sing along with the melody as well if you feel like it. Clap, stamp, jump, wave your arms about. As Richard Moss says, 'It is possible to let your whole body become a celebration.' If you can, keep going for about twenty minutes or until the end of the record. Then lie down with your knees bent and your feet flat on the ground, place your hands over your abdomen and breathe deeply for a few minutes. Enjoy the sense of energy in your body.

This merging and dissolving with the music is a very simple but extremely valuable tool for bringing ourselves to a sense of ease and unity, harmonizing ourselves with the universe and enjoying a sense of fun and play at the same time.

Music list – some personal suggestions

Wagner	The *Siegfried Idyll*
	Parsifal
	Gotterdammung (selections)
Bach	Unaccompanied cello
	The 6 Brandenberg Concertos
	Double violin concerto
	Magnificat
	Cantata – *Sleepers Awake*
	St Matthew Passion
Schubert	Piano quintet
	String Quartet no. 14 in D Minor
	String Quartet no. 15 in G Major
Debussy	String quartet
	"Claire de Lune"
Elgar	Cello concerto
	Violin concerto
	Serenade for Strings op. 20 in E Minor
Dvorak	Cello concerto
	New World Symphony
Mozart	*Requiem*
	Clarinet concerto
	Flute Concertos no. 1 on G Major, no. 2 in D Major
	Andante for Flute and Orchestra in C Major
	Piano concertos nos. 17 and 21
Beethoven	Symphony no. 7
	Symphony no. 9
Vivaldi	*The Four Seasons*
Verdi	*Requiem*
Pachelbel	Canon
Barber	Introduction and Allegro for Strings
Brahms	Symphony no. 1
	Piano trio
Albinoni	Adagio for Strings and Organ
Handel	*Messiah*
Bruckner	Symphony no. 9

Sibelius	*The Swan of Tuonella*
Ravel	*Pavanne for a Dead Infanta*
	Mother Goose Suite
	String quartet
	Daphnis and Chloe
Fauré	*Requiem*
Stravinsky	*Symphony of Psalms*
	The Firebird
	The Rite of Spring
Rachmaninov	Symphony no. 1
	Piano Concertos 1, 2 and 3
Vaughan Williams	"Variations on a Theme by Thomas Tallis"
	"The Lark Ascending"

Indian classical music, e.g. ragas played by Ravi Shankar, Ram Narayan, Budhaditya Mukherjee etc

The Gyuto Monks	"Tibetan Tantric"
	"Freedom Chants"
Paul Horn	"Inside the Great Pyramid"
	"Inside the Taj Mahal"
✓ Coyote Oldman	"Tear of the Moon"
Gene Groeschel	"Hawk Eyes Dreaming"
Daniel Kobialka	"Timeless Motion"
Michael Stearns	"Planetary Unfolding"
Rusty Crutcher	"Macchu Picchu Impressions"
Aswad	"A New Chapter of Dub"
Steel Pulse	"True Democracy"
Enigma	"MCMXC A.D."
Moving Hearts	"The Storm"
Enya	"Watermark"
Sade	"Diamond Life"
Sachdev	"Master of the Bamboo Flute"
Vangelis	"Antarctica"
Songs of the Humpback Whale	
Environments	"Slow Ocean"
Scott Fitzgerald	"Thunderdrums"
Flying Monkey Orchestra	"Dig"

84

Mark Robson	"A Celtic Dreaming"
Paul Winter	"Canyon"
Tim Wheater	"Awakenings"
Larkin	"O'cean"

Gregorian chants sung by the Benedictine Nuns of
  St Cecelia's Abbey, Isle of Wight

Miles Davis	"Kind of Blue"
Getz/Gilberto	"Brazilian Sambas"
The Gypsy Kings	Music from the Russian Orthodox Church
Palestrina	Missa *Papa Marcello*
Byrd	Mass in 4 parts
	Mass in 5 parts
Rodriquez	Guitar concerto
Also jazz version	"Concierto," played by Jim Hall

6
LOOKING AFTER YOUR BODY

Men occasionally stumble over the Truth, but most pick
themselves up and hurry off as if nothing had
happened.

Winston Churchill

Everyone has access to mystical and spiritual knowledge.
The rate at which we grow spiritually, however, depends
upon our level of commitment. Laeh Maggie Garfield in
her book *Sound Medicine* reminds us humorously what
commitment means: 'As in the example of a ham and eggs
breakfast', she writes, 'the chicken is involved but the pig
is committed. Commitment is the single most influential
ingredient in spiritual growth. Without it, you're just
another tourist exploring the inner landscape.'

Commitment is so *difficult* though. Change is frightening. We hang on to the comfort of old patterns no
matter how destructive they are rather than risk the
unknown and the fear of failure. If we weren't challenged
by crisis or illness we would probably never change
anything.

A healthy body is one whose elements are in balance
and, of course, the world around us contains all the
nutrients we require for a healthy and balanced life. It's
just doing it! A large part of self-healing consists of a
determination to tackle this fundamental area of personal
responsibility.

After my confrontation with cancer, I knew that a major
factor in getting well again would be a change in the eating
habits of a lifetime – an unhappy relationship with food
and a recurrent pattern of dieting and bingeing. Right

86

from day one after the operation I decided to go on a healthy eating programme to detoxify my body, to minimize the traumatic effects of the surgery and radiotherapy and to boost my immune system.

When your life has seemingly been overtaken by catastrophe you feel very powerless, at the mercy of a medical profession which for all its cleverness has the tendency to reduce you to a passive, docile 'patient'. Getting in the driving seat again is an essential part of recovery.

In order for energy to be transformed from one state to another it must be in a constant flow through the body. In a healthy, active rhythm, the positive and negative forces which constantly push and pull us are in a balanced state – the state known as homeostasis. My dictionary defines this as: 'the maintenance of metabolic equilibrium within an animal by a tendency to compensate for disruptive changes'. Quite often we do not choose what is suitable for our growth and balanced maintenance. We ignore the disruptive changes. A perverted form of homeostasis – addiction – takes over. We dull the pain with food, with alcohol, with drugs and pills, with destructive relationships. Blockages in the vital flow of energy occur, the rhythm becomes erratic. Ill health is the alarm system, and putting effort into your diet always brings rewards. Be prepared to experiment with what suits your body, come to terms with it and take heed. Diet is not the total answer to healing, but without a good diet there is no answer.

DETOXIFICATION

First a brief word of warning here – fanaticism is rarely a healthy phenomenon and becoming obsessive, humourless or dogmatic about diet is counterproductive. There is enormous ethnic variety within the parameter of human norms and not everybody can assimilate the same foods in the same way. The descendant of a Masai tribesman, a Vietnamese fisherman and a Hassidic Jew have probably inherited constitutional differences even though they all may live in London and work at similar jobs. Common-sense and making allowances for individual differences should always temper any general rule. Also, if you are very underweight, be sure to get medical advice before undertaking this.

So saying, whether you are coping with cancer or some other life-threatening or chronic disease or whether you would just like to do your body a favour and make a fresh start, a good cleansing of the digestive system is a wonderful way to begin. It is a gesture of goodwill and intention towards your body and your life. It is the first step in that vital 'commitment'. Attitude is very important here. A joyful, adventurous, hopeful frame of mind will multiply the benefits. If you are feeling resentful and deprived you will be wasting your time. Your body will get only negative messages and be counting the minutes until it can subvert your efforts.

If the weather is warm, begin with a three-day grape mono-diet, eating as many grapes as you want and drinking only pure water, herb teas and grape juice. If the weather is cold, have brown rice and vegetable broth instead.

This has the effect of cleaning your digestive tract and making you very sensitive to the way your body reacts to each new food as you add it.

I would also just like to plant the idea of finding out about colonic irrigation. I mention this rather *sotto voce* because some people are appalled at the idea and have long memories of ghastly enemas in childhood. However, under proper supervision, a good cleanse of the organs of elimination can have a remarkable effect on your feeling of well-being. Do-it-yourself coffee enemas may sound hilarious but they stimulate the liver, the major organ of detoxification, and help to eliminate old, clogged fecal matter from the colon. I am a recent convert and, like everyone else I know who has tried them, I felt an immediate benefit. Ian Gawler, in his helpful book, *You Can Conquer Cancer*, says they are also remarkably effective in combating and relieving pain. He cured himself of advanced bone cancer.

Then for two weeks try a light vegetarian diet. Most people find doing without dairy products, eggs and meat makes them feel a lot better straight away. Drink lots of freshly squeezed fruit and vegetable juices. A juice extractor is a really worthwhile investment. Eat as many raw foods as you can and buy organic produce if at all possible. So many of our modern illnesses must be at least partly attributable to modern farming methods with their high emphasis on pesticides, artificial fertilizers and the large amounts of antibiotics, hormones and steroids given to the animals we eat.

Be mindful of getting enough energy from carbohydrates – wholemeal bread and pasta, porridge, legumes, potatoes, sweet potatoes. These also provide valuable fibre and, contrary to popular assumption, are not fattening unless consumed with lashings of butter. When you cook things try to steam or bake them instead of frying. Avoid butter and margarine altogether, using only cold-pressed extra virgin olive oil for salad dressing.

If you are convinced that you are not one of life's natural vegetarians, you can introduce fish and free range chicken later on, but since animal protein takes much longer to digest, it's a good idea to leave it out while you are giving your system a rest. After the first couple of weeks, you can also add up to two glasses of wine a day if you like it. It has the effect of cheering you up and making the diet seem less punitive as well as being a good source of iron.

The real villains of the piece are sugar (especially refined sugar), caffeine, too much salt, refined flour, chemical additives and processed foods. Really try to eliminate these from your life. However, if once in a while you long for an ice-cream or a pink cake – have one but eat it consciously, with sensuous enjoyment and gusto rather than guilt!

Thereafter, listen to your body and the 'maintenance of metabolic equilibrium' will take care of itself. The pro-immunity, vitality-producing foods are contained in the table on p. 91, adapted from *Maximum Immunity* by

Michael A. Weiner. If you keep this as the basic eating framework of your life, then you can relax about those times when you are invited out to friends or want to have a meal in a restaurant. In other words, no harm will be done if you occasionally stray from the path. You can be flexible and make allowances for those times when the food you eat is not what you would have chosen.

SUPPLEMENTS

There is a constant debate going on about the merits or otherwise of taking vitamin and mineral supplements. One argument is that if you are eating a balanced diet you shouldn't need them and all you end up with is expensive urine. The other is that since everyone's needs are different and also vary a lot in the course of their lifetime, it is quite difficult to know if you are getting enough. Sometimes, you may well need a boost. I strongly recommend getting professional advice here. I followed the revised Bristol Cancer Help Centre programme of immuno-friendly diet plus supplementary vitamins and minerals and felt wonderful on it. As Michael Weiner writes in *Maximum Immunity*, 'The point ... is to emphasize the powers of nature and make the link to our own natural healers within. Instead of seeking *outside* of our bodies for healing properties, we should conceptualize the pharmacy within and clearly see that by providing the shelves with the necessary compounds in the form of required nutrients, we can use our mind to make the inner drugs. That is the story of natural healing.'

EXERCISE

The body's influence on the mind is just as important as the mind's influence on the body. Exercise, in the West, always has a faintly punitive and spartan connotation like horrible-tasting medicine. It's good for you but something to be got over with as quickly as possible. The joy isn't in the doing of it but in the righteous feeling of having done it.

Basic eating framework

Food category	Recommended foods
Beverages	Herb teas (e.g. chamomile, mint, papaya; no caffeine), fresh fruit and vegetable juices.
Dairy products	Goats' milk or soya milk, live yoghurt, non-fat cottage cheese, goats' or sheep cheese.
Eggs	Free range, poached or soft-boiled, not more than four a week.
Fruit	All dried (unsulphured), stewed, fresh, and frozen (unsweetened).
Grains	Whole-grain cereals, bread, muffins (e.g. rye, oats, bran, buckwheat, millet), brown rice, whole seeds (sesame, pumpkin, sunflower, flaxseed).
Meat	The less the better. Particularly avoid processed meats (e.g. sausages, frankfurters, salami, bacon and others preserved with nitrates).
Fish	Fresh, white-fleshed, grilled or baked.
Nuts	All fresh, raw or lightly roasted (unsalted) except peanuts. High fat content.
Oils	Cold-pressed olive oil.
Seasonings	Herbs, plenty (grow your own if you can), rosemary, marjoram, garlic, ginger, sage, thyme, fennel. Go easy on hot spices and salt.
Sprouts	The fresher the better, easy to grow at home (e.g. wheat grass, pea, lentil, mung). For salads or stir-fries.
Sweets	Pure, unfiltered honey, unsulphured molasses, date syrup, maple syrup (in limited amounts only).

Vegetables	All raw or lightly steamed, quick stir-fried, or baked.
Tofu or bean curd	This is a wonderful source of complete protein containing all the essential amino acids. It is low in sodium and fat and can be prepared in many creative ways, with a variety of flavours and textures. The Japanese and Chinese have used this food since antiquity.

Miserable-looking joggers plodding along in a light drizzle seem to exemplify this attitude. Like diet, if you're not getting any enjoyment whatsoever from it, it's probably not going to do you much good.

Regular exercise is known to be an important factor in maintaing a balanced equilibrium but perhaps the Eastern view of it is a better one to adopt. There it is seen as something to be engaged in and enjoyed for its own sake, as time out from the cares of daily life, a treat. Think of the real meaning of the word 're-creation'. It is a wonderful sight to see elderly Chinese in the park doing their t'ai chi, opening out like waterlilies in the early morning sunshine.

Once again, intelligent caution and moderation are the watchwords here. A sudden outburst of competitive squash or marathon running will not protect you against a heart attack; it's more likely to give you one. Exercise needs to be part of a complete programme which includes nutrition and psychological well-being. If you are overweight, over forty, unfit or recovering from an illness, seek medical advice.

Try to include some *vigorous* exercise, in the fresh air if possible, such as brisk walking, jogging (only if you enjoy it!), cycling, dancing or swimming; some *strengthening* exercise such as Callanetics, Jane Fonda or Rosemary Conley methods (available on video), working out at a gym or gardening; and some *flexibility* exercise, stretching and bending, yoga or t'ai chi.

MEDITATION

To balance all this activity, the third leg of the tripod is meditation. Spiritually, many people find that it leads to a peace of mind they had not imagined possible. There is an excellent short introduction to the subject in *Meditation* by Erica Smith and Nicholas Wilks (see Further Reading at back) so I won't go into detail here. Suffice to say that although many of the benefits of meditation are already contained in the practices of visualization and listening to music that we've already spoken about, pure meditation, in the sense of emptying the mind, has a special quality all of its own.

Someone once said, 'Prayer is talking; meditation is listening.' It is about opening your inner eyes to see what was there all along. Our higher wisdom is not 'out there', it is within us. In fact, according to Buddhist thinking, it is only our cock-eyed concepts that create boundaries between inner and outer in the first place.

Meditation enables us to stop being prey to the constant pressures and distractions of everyday life and to acknowledge other, more profound things – our deeper thoughts and feelings, the peace of pure consciousness, and spiritual awareness.

Stress, as we now know, is a major factor in the development of disease. If you suffer from stress, one of the most obvious signals in your body will be physical tension. When your stomach is knotted, your brow knitted, your shoulders rigid, your jaw clamped, your hands clenched – beware! You are heading for trouble.

Whenever you are called upon to face a challenge in your life, your body reacts to the stimulus by producing chemical changes. Among other responses adrenalin is released and the body beefed up for a fight or flight response. If action is thwarted or the situation unresolved, the cycle is incomplete and the chemical changes remain in the body. This leads to physical tension and lowered immunity. Sounds familiar? Modern life throws up dozens of these frustrations daily; can't get through on the phone, problems at work, someone steals your handbag, the kids track mud on the carpet, the car in front gets the last parking meter, you sit in a traffic jam knowing you've missed the plane ... the list is endless.

Add to this time and the interaction of other negative factors and you become a seething volcano of poisonous gases – a combustion engine with a cork stuck in the exhaust pipe. The stresses accumulate and the inevitable outcome is disease. Once again the temptation is to have a drink or a pill, but nothing works as effectively as regular meditation. It is the easiest, safest, most reliable method for relieving muscular tension and stress. By achieving a state of inner stillness meditation gives you the means of releasing stress whatever its original cause. Short regular periods can prevent stress from reaching dangerous levels. Longer periods can actually undo the damage and get you back on the road to health again.

Essentially it works because it stills the active, thinking brain and allows the creative, intuitive side to come into its own. Significantly, the very act of trying too hard will often result in failure. Only by abandoning our usual sense of striving and achievement, by surrendering and trusting for a change, do we allow ourselves to be open, really open, to the principles of change. We are so used to struggling for things that it's quite difficult to learn that meditation works best when it's effortless. All you need to do is make time for it.

With guidance and patience, meditation can lead to breathtaking experiences of cosmic at-oneness and enlightenment, but don't expect anything startling to begin with. The first changes you notice will be gentle and subtle. Your concentration will improve, you won't be so irritable or paranoid. The deep, restful calm actually strengthens your mental powers by freeing the mind from its accustomed turmoil. Rudolph Steiner once said, 'Knowledge is received only in those moments in which every judgement, every criticism coming from ourselves is silent.'

The physical benefits of meditation have been well known in the East for hundreds of years but Western science has only just begun to research its effects on the disease process. What is already apparent is the role of meditation in reducing blood pressure, producing changes in brain wave patterns, raising levels of white blood cells and thereby improving the efficiency of the immune system.

Emotionally, people find they feel better about themselves, they feel more able to accept their strengths and limitations, more able to relate to others in an open, honest way. As Bernie Siegel says, meditation helps you grow up. It leads to greater capacity for loving, both self-love and compassion for others. People find they are able to give of themselves more freely and so be of more help to those around them.

All you need in order to bring this magnificently simple tool into your life is the commitment to give it 20 minutes a day. (I am actually talking to myself here. I *know* how much I love meditation and how good it makes me feel, but woeful lack of self-discipline has led to a whole string of convincing excuses as to why I never get round to it. I will, and that's a promise.)

Until I had learned how to meditate, I'd never really understood the concept of emptiness. We are afraid of our own spaciousness because it makes us feel insubstantial, so we keep trying to fill it with things. Entering into the void is an act of communion with our true nature. It is the spark of divinity, which we are, merging with the flame, the drop rejoining the ocean. In meditation, the questing, questioning mind expands to a place where the need to understand is no longer important. As you let go of comparisons and judgements and attachments, you can experience the pure nature of mind itself.

Reading a good book on the subject or doing a TM (transcendental meditation) course is a good way to get started, otherwise the main things you need to do are just to sit comfortably in a quiet place, close your eyes and focus your attention on the breath. As it is very difficult to think of nothing at all, it is quite helpful to keep the thinking mind occupied with counting the breaths, slowly from one to ten over and over again. When thoughts or images try to distract you, just notice them and let them go. Bring your awareness gently back to the breath and start counting from one again.

Silently repeating a mantra or sacred sound is another popular way to keep the active mind, the guard dog, occupied while you sneak past to the infinity beyond.

Enjoy the spaciousness.

7
SOME HEALING REMEDIES FOR COMMON AILMENTS

It is in the nature of the body to heal itself. Cells will regenerate and heal themselves quickly if given a favourable environment. 'Spontaneous remission' is a phrase used rather dismissively by doctors when they can't explain what happened. It means the disease went away by itself without any medical intervention. It is one of those astonishing events like the placebo effect which attests to the body's ability to heal itself.

I often wonder why the medical profession isn't more interested in this miraculous phenomenon. Doctors are inclined to say, impatiently, as my consultant did, 'There's absolutely no proof that so-called "healing" works. It's all in the mind. It's nothing but pure imagination. Spontaneous remissions just sometimes happen of their own accord, that's all.' Why aren't they asking the really interesting questions such as: 'What is pure imagination? Who are these people who have spontaneous remissions? What is going on in their lives? What happened to their immune systems to cause such a dramatic change?' Bernie Siegel asks these and other refreshing questions in his seminal book, *Love, Medicine and Miracles*.

Healing works at a cellular level, by helping to create a favourable environment in which miracles are quite compatible with the laws of nature. Miracles are very ordinary and happen all the time. Cuts mend, burns heal, bleeding stops, bones knit, fluids lubricate, waste products expel themselves, the body maintains a constant temperature, new life grows from seed.

A favourable environment includes proper nourishment, proper rest and relaxation, laughter and play, positive thoughts and actions, some knowledge of the help available to us through nature, and the chance both to give and receive unconditional love. This last item often provides the stumbling block. If love becomes blocked, the organism goes into a nose dive. Love and the life-force are intimately connected.

In the preceding chapters I have tried to present an array of everyday things available to all of us to use for self-healing and healing others. The same qualities are needed for both – a willingness to be a channel through which the life energy can flow and an attitude of non-judgemental compassion. Sometimes it is very hard to apply the latter towards ourselves and yet the attitude we have towards ourselves is the single most important factor in healing or staying well. As Bernie Siegel has said, it sometimes takes a life-threatening illness to get you to wake up and live. If it takes the knowledge that we won't live for ever to make life worth living, why are we so afraid to love? When we choose to love, healing energy is released in our bodies.

So saying, in this chapter I include a few techniques and procedures which have proved successful many times for the home treatment of common ailments. It's a bit of a hodge-podge, but I hope you will add to these from other sources and develop your own personal collection. A book on homeopathic remedies, Bach flower remedies and a good old-fashioned herbal are a useful addition to anyone's shelves, and I always keep a bottle of Bach's Rescue Remedy (see p. 115) both in the house and in my handbag for emergencies.

First a word about healing and the law. Remember that in all cases we are seeking to augment and complement the work of the medical profession. Healers are not qualified to give medical advice or to interfere in any way between doctor and patient. Nobody should ever be persuaded to disregard the doctor's advice. You should also know that it is a criminal offence for a parent or guardian to fail to provide adequate medical aid for a child under 16. Healing is not medical aid as defined by law, and a healer who treats a child whose parents refuse medical aid runs the risk of aiding and abetting that offence. This doesn't mean that you refuse to give healing to children, only that you make sure to advise the parents of the law.

SOME HEALING REMEDIES

Begin all these treatments by centering yourself and silently asking the patient's higher self for permission to intervene.

Treatment for a tension headache

Get your patient to sit on a straight-backed chair and stand behind her. (If you are the one with the headache, you can do this on yourself but it is even better to get a friend to do it for you.) Put a small dab of undiluted lavender essential oil on each temple and using the middle finger of each hand massage gently but firmly for a few minutes. Next rub your hands briskly together and gently place the palm of your right hand on the back of the person's neck and the palm of your left hand about half and inch from her forehead. (Remember, the right hand is the 'transmitter' and the left hand the 'receiver'. You are literally pulling the pain out – see Fig. 19.)

Ask her to take 10 deep breaths and let each one out with a sigh. Synchronize your breathing with hers, then just remain there quietly as long as you feel the energy flowing. Usually 3 to 5 minutes is enough and most headaches will be completely gone. I like to follow this up by offering a homemade herbal tea which is wonderful for headaches and nervousness:

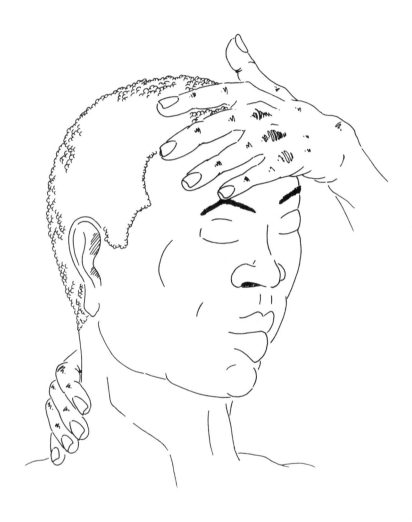

Fig. 19 Relieving a tension headache

To 1 pint of boiling water add:
1 tsp valerian
2 tsps chamomile
½ stick of liquorice root, bruised in a mortar.
Steep for 10 to 15 minutes.
Drink from a nice china cup if possible.

After a healing, drink a glass of water yourself and wash your hands under running water to remove the excess energy.

Stiffness in the neck and shoulders
Place one hand flat on the solar plexus, just below the rib cage, and the other with your fingers spread out along the neck vertebrae as if you were playing the piano. Hold for about 5 minutes. People invariably report a feeling of ease and warmth. A few drops of essential oil of rosemary in a burner and a gentle massage of the painful area with some oil to which a few drops of rosemary have been added also works wonders.

Joint pains and arthritis
Place your left hand tenderly on or above the painful area and your right hand on the heart chakra. Hold for about five minutes. A gentle massage with a little oil to which a pinch of cayenne pepper has been added often brings relief, particularly to arthritic hands.
Castor oil packs overnight are also excellent for painful joints. Cut a piece of white plastic to size (a plain supermarket carrier bag will do.) Next, cut a piece of white cotton or linen the same size (or use a cotton handkerchief). Wet this by wringing it out in water and lay it on top of the plastic. Finally, cut a piece of white towelling to size or use a washcloth and lay it on the wet linen. On this you drizzle about 50 ml castor oil (see Fig. 20). Before going to bed, place on the painful area, castor oil side down, and secure firmly with an elastic bandage. The outer layers stop the oil soaking through the wrong way. In the morning you will be amazed that the oil has been almost completely

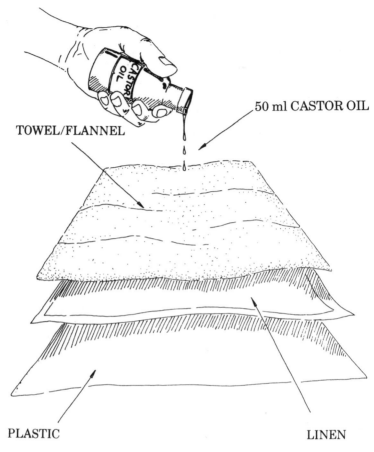

50 ml CASTOR OIL

TOWEL/FLANNEL

PLASTIC

LINEN

Fig. 20 Making a castor oil pack

absorbed into the skin. You are literally oiling the joints. The pack can be re-used many times, replenishing the castor oil as it soaks in. Any excess oil on the skin can be cleaned off with a little baking soda in warm water.

A week of alternating the packs with the laying-on-of-hands healing brings relief in most cases. If you are applying the packs for someone, hold your hands gently around the bandaged area for a few minutes sending healing energy. To do this for an elderly relative would be a practical, effective way of providing comfort and showing love and concern.

Colour visualization breathing

Do this for yourself or suggest it to the person you are healing to be used in conjunction with a simple energy transference.

Lie down in a warm, comfortable room and, choosing a colour helpful to the condition you wish to treat, visualize it as a cloud which you slowly inhale through the fingers and toes, imagining them hollow, imagining your whole body porous to the breath. The radiantly coloured breath then travels upwards, through your hollow bones, just beneath the surface of the skin, rising in a spiral about the body and ending above the head in a brilliant swirl (see Fig. 21). Then as you exhale, feel the coloured breath pass out through the pores of the skin carrying all impurities with it. This sounds complicated but it is very easy to do and a very effective way of using the power of the mind to stimulate and strengthen the recuperative processes.

Colour breathing visualization has many applications. The therapeutic properties of the colours, according to healer, Jack Schwartz, are as follows:

Red: Good for circulation, blood ailments, sexual dysfunction, and paralysis.

Orange: Good for lactation, pulse rate, dispelling kidney stones and gallstones, hernias, depression, appendicitis.

Yellow: Energy for the lymphatic system, good for indigestion, diabetes, kidney and liver ailments, constipation, some eye and throat conditions.

Green: Good for nervous conditions, hay fever, ulcers, influenza, syphilis, malaria, colds.

Turquoise: Anti-inflammatory, good for throat problems.

Blue: For pain relief, bleeding, healing burns (excellent to use during a course of radiotherapy), treating dysentery, colic, respiratory problems, skin troubles, rheumatism.

Indigo: Cataracts, migraine, deafness, skin dis-
             orders, soothing effect on eyes, ears, nervous
             system.
Violet: Good for emotional problems, arthritis,
             easing childbirth.
Magenta: Good for heart and mental problems.

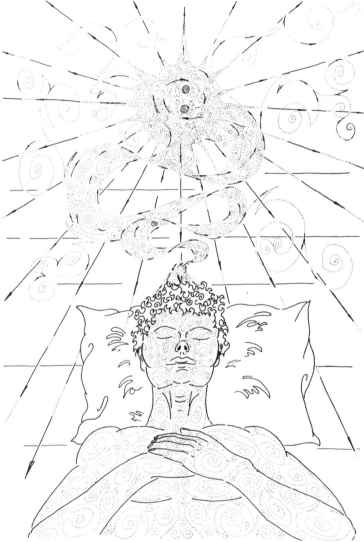

Fig. 21 Colour visualization breathing

A treatment for lower back pain

If at all possible, have the patient curl up in a fetal position or, better still, in the yoga position known as the pose of a child. Rub your hands briskly together and place side by side directly on the lower back. Hold in place for about five minutes sending love and warmth into the area. (If you're keen to try the use of music, you might choose something like the slow movement of Brahms's Piano Quartet in C Minor Op. 60) Next, I would use a crystal, holding the flatter end firmly in the palm of my hand and circling it a few inches above the painful area, first in an

Fig. 22 The pose of a child

105

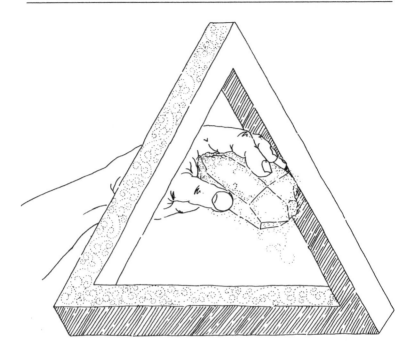

Fig. 23 Holding a crystal in the left hand to take out pain. Transfer to the right hand to put healing in.

anticlockwise motion for a few minutes (to take out pain), then in a clockwise motion, again for a few minutes (to put healing in).

To relieve lower back pain in yourself, it often helps enormously to lie down with a couple of books under your head to ensure that your neck is straight, pressing the small of your back into the floor with your knees bent and your feet flat on the ground. Keeping your shoulders flat, let your knees drop over first to one side then the other. Then centre them again and with the hands clasped loosely over the solar plexus, stay there for about 15 minutes. This is one of the basic positions used in Alexander technique, a method of re-aligning the body to release stored tension (see Fig. 24). Finally, get into the pose of a child and massage your lower back gently with the knuckles of both hands.

Fig. 24 Basic relaxation position

I am aware that all this sounds rather far-fetched. I only hope you are intrigued enough to try it for yourself before you dismiss it as nonsense. Once you have experienced this gentle, natural healing you will never feel helpless again. Whatever treatment you are having from your doctor, it can be complemented and augmented by these simple procedures or they can be used as first aid. Reclaiming our power to help each other and help ourselves is a crucial cornerstone of holistic thinking.

A comfort healing

I have used this for people following a bereavement or emotional trauma. It is also wonderful for children before bedtime.

Have your patient lie down flat on his back with cushions under the knees of necessary. Stand or sit on his right side. Rub your hands briskly together and place them on either side of the abdomen for a minute or so. Then place the left hand on the forehead and the right hand just below the navel. Gently but firmly rock the person from side to side with your right hand for a few minutes and, finally, leaving your hands in place, stop rocking and just continue transmitting the energy into the abdomen for as long as it seems appropriate (see Fig. 25). Gradually withdraw your hands and stroke the entire auric field in a smooth downward motion a few times. This could be an occasion to try some humming if the idea appeals to you, particularly with children.

Fig. 25 Giving a comfort healing

Healing scar tissue

First, break open a capsule of vitamin E oil (or use a vitamin E ointment) and massage it into the area gently with the tips of your fingers. It's important to focus your thoughts on the knowledge that scar tissue can soften and be replaced by flexible, living tissue and that damaged nerves can heal and grow again. Visualize images of life and vitality: pale green ferns uncurling, new shoots unfurling, sea water swirling, micro-organisms dancing, the whole process of creation happening before your eyes. Rub your hands briskly together and either place them directly on the scar or a couple of inches above it channelling energy.

A man came to me once for healing. A very practical, 'action man' type of chap, he had been very sceptical of the whole idea but his wife had persuaded him to try it. Three months before, he had fallen through a glass skylight while mending his roof and had practically severed his left leg. The surgeons had done a wonderful job of stitching him back together, but the leg was like a dead white fish. No sensation, no movement and a horrendous scar. We worked on the visualization together and I sat on the floor and held his foot in my hands.

After about ten minutes he began to have a strong sensation of pins and needles in the bad foot. We were both so excited we could hardly contain ourselves. Before our eyes the lifeless flesh turned pink and that was the beginning of a remarkable recovery. I showed his wife how to do the simple healing transaction and, once having decided to commit himself to the visualizations, the man threw himself into the endeavour with his customary vigour.

The neuro-surgeons at the hospital were amazed at the rapid rate of nerve growth and within a relatively short time he was walking unaided. The scar faded to a barely perceptible thread and about a year after the accident I had a telephone call from him saying, 'I thought you might like to know that this morning I went out jogging for three miles!'

Accelerated bone healing

Bones respond very well to the use of sound, low-pitched wind instruments in particular such as the bassoon, Andean flute or didgeridoo. Place the fingertips of both hands very lightly on the bone and try to get an image in your mind of all the layers beneath your fingers: skin, fat, muscle, the thin layer of fibrous tissue which envelops the bone (the periosteum), the compact outer surface of the bone, the porous, spongy inner bone, the bone marrow in the cavity (see Fig. 26).

The periosteum is a source of cells for bone growth and repair so focus on this in particular. Feel the life-force energy like thin beams of light pouring down your arms, spreading out through your fingers, penetrating deep into the body, stirring up the cells, accelerating the healing response. Keep your hands in position for about 10 to 15 minutes then take two crystals and hold them in place at either end of the bone with both the pointed ends facing towards the head like two batteries in a torch. You can do this while a limb is still in plaster and also when it comes out (see Fig. 27).

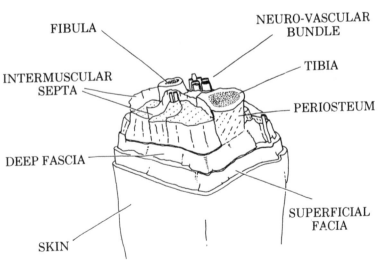

Fig. 26 Be aware of the many layers beneath your hands when you give healing to a bone.

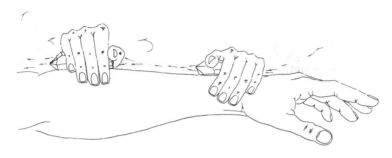

Fig. 27 Using crystals for bone healing

Coping with emotions

Quite often, during the course of a healing, a person might begin to feel emotions welling up. The atmosphere of acceptance and trust has made it acceptable to be vulnerable. It's not at all unusual to feel tearful and it's a very encouraging indication that the person feels safe. Sometimes just the recognition that someone is listening to them and giving them time and attention is enough to open the floodgates. Years of suppression have created a huge lake of unshed tears dammed up behind a wall of good manners and civilized niceties. The tears are for the buried grief and pain of a lifetime, for the little child within who has had such a hard time.

Our society is very ill at ease with the expression of emotions. Most of us have been taught that it is babyish to cry and shows appalling lack of control. Christopher Spence, director of London Lighthouse, the organization for people with AIDS, once said, 'If all the tears of the suburbs were shed, it would never stop raining.'

It is a very sacred honour to be entrusted with someone's tears. Don't worry that you won't know what to do. You don't have to do anything. In fact you are already doing it; you have found a way to reach out and touch. Don't be afraid or embarrassed. Don't say, 'there, there don't cry', or you will only reinforce the old proscriptions.

The tears are very healing. Just be there and keep a box of tissues handy. You can't make it different, you can't change the past, but you can be a witness. You can stand steady and accompany the person on the journey.

Also, people often feel bad and guilty that they have taken so long to get to the point of seeking healing. It's important for them to understand that they did the best they knew how with the choices that were available to them. Now their innate wisdom knows that they no longer have to be limited by the same choices and they are free to widen their horizons. The tears are often tears of relief. The role of the healer is to help create a space where change is possible. Trust this process. Remember, you are not perfect but you are enough and you are there.

Bach flower remedies

There are thirty-eight of these little preparations made under strict supervision from Dr Edward Bach's original formulae using wild plants and trees from the countryside. They work in a similar way to homeopathic remedies at the subtle level of vibrational frequencies. They are for treating the person not the disease, the cause not the effect, and can be classified into seven groups according to the predominant emotion.

Bach flower remedies are completely safe. Choose one or more remedies from the characteristics that you feel best describe the patient and mix up a little dropper bottle with a few drops of each in some pure spring water and half a teaspoon of brandy. The remedies work slowly and gently so need to be taken regularly for a period of a few weeks: five or six drops on the tongue or in a glass of water sipped slowly three times a day. They are a lovely extra tool to have and can be bought from good natural food stores and drugstores that carry homeopathic products. The remedies can have a dramatic influence, improving patients' general attitude, helping them to feel cared for and understood, and therefore helping with their physical recovery.

Bach flower remedies

Predominant emotion	Negative aspects treated
FEAR	
Rock Rose*	Extreme fear, terror, panic.
Mimulus	Shyness, timidity, fear of specific things (e.g. meeting people, speaking in public).
Cherry Plum*	Fear of loss of control, doing harm to others, violent temper.
Aspen	Apprehension, fear that something terrible will happen, sense of foreboding.
Red Chestnut	Anxiety and fear for others (especially loved ones).
UNCERTAINTY	
Cerato	Doubts own judgement.
Scleranthus	Indecision, fluctuating moods.
Gentian	Easily discouraged, despondent, negative.
Gorse	Hopelessness and pessimism.
Hornbeam	Procrastinates.
Wild oat	Unfulfilled, doesn't know what he wants to do or how to get started.
LACK OF INTEREST	
Clematis*	Daydreamy, absent-minded, escapist.
Honeysuckle	Nostalgic, lives in the past, homesick.
Wild Rose	Apathetic, resigned, lacking in ambition.
Olive	Lethargic, drained of energy, everything is an effort.
White Chestnut	Chronic worrier, plagued with persistent unwanted thoughts and mental arguments.

Mustard	Gloom and melancholia, sudden dark cloud descends for no known reason.
Chestnut Bud	Repeats same mistakes, doesn't learn from experience.

LONELINESS

Water Violet	Proud, reserved, aloof, independent, finds it difficult to ask for help.
Impatiens*	Impatient, intolerant, hasty, irritable.
Heather	Egocentric bore, compulsive talker, hates to be alone.

OVERSENSITIVITY TO INFLUENCES AND IDEAS

Holly	Lacking in love for others, jealous, envious, vengeful, paranoid, suspicious.
Walnut	For rites of passage (e.g. puberty, menopause), helps adjust to change.
Centaury	Weak-willed, anxious to please, 'doormat' tendency, unable to say 'no'.
Agrimony	Inner torment behind a facade of cheerfulness, hides worries from others.

DESPONDENCY AND DESPAIR

Crab Apple	Self-disgust, feels unclean, ashamed, often excessively houseproud.
Oak	Normally brave and determined but no longer able to struggle on.
Willow	Resentful, bitter, self-pitying.
Star of Bethlehem*	For the effect of shock, bad news, great sorrow, trauma.
Sweet Chestnut	Extreme anguish, reached the limits of endurance.
Elm	Normally very capable, temporary feelings of being overwhelmed by responsibilities and unable to cope.

Pine	Guilt, self-reproach, over-conscientious, takes the blame for others' mistakes.
Larch	No confidence, gives up easily, feels inferior, anticipates failure.

EXCESSIVE CONCERN WITH WHAT'S BEST FOR OTHERS

Rock Water	Self-righteous, rigid in outlook, self-denying.
Beech	Intolerant, critical, arrogant, judgemental.
Vine	Domineering, autocratic, inflexible, ambitious, tyrannical.
Vervain	Fanatical, incensed by injustice, highly strung.
Chicory	Possessive, selfish, demands respect and obedience.

Rescue Remedy: A ready-mixed combination of the five remedies (starred above): Cherry Plum, Clematis, Impatiens, Rock Rose, and Star of Bethlehem for use in emergencies and accidents. Very powerful first aid. Available as a liquid in a dropper bottle or as a cream for burns, cuts, stings and bites. Completely safe for use with children or animals.

Tissue salts

Another useful collection of remedies to have to hand are the twelve inorganic chemical compounds or homoeopathic 'tissue salts' identified by Dr William Schuessler. The theory is that any deficiencies in these substances result in the body's inability to repair itself. A book on homoeopathy will give you more information but for the time being it is enough to know that very small doses of the required tissue salts can help put the body on the road to recovery. Again these remedies work at a very subtle level and are diluted to such low potencies that it only makes sense to think of them having an effect as vibrational frequencies. For home prescription, do not take remedies of a higher potency than 30.

Tissue salts

Common name	Effect
Calcium fluoride	Strengthens tissue.
Calcium phosphate	Improves health of bones, prevents haemorrhaging.
Calcium sulphate	Good for reproductive organs, hay fever, skin problems.
Iron phosphate	Oxygenates blood, copes with inflammation.
Potassium chloride	Stimulates cells and helps with inflammation.
Potassium phosphate	Aids nervous system, tones muscles and stops degeneration.
Potassium sulphate	Oxygenates cells, maintains healthy skin and nails.
Magnesium phosphate	Enables cells to eliminate waste, relaxes muscles, good for insomnia.
Sodium chloride	Good for circulation, arthritic and rheumatic pain, regulates distribution of water.
Sodium phosphate	Neutralizes lactic acid, helps prevent cholesterol, good for indigestion.
Sodium phosphate	Stimulates bile, balances level of water in the body.

Silicone dioxide	Removes excess calcium, good for arthritis, eliminates pus.

I want to emphasize that you do not need to know all this in order to be an effective healer. The simple laying-on-of-hands is the starting point and may well be all you will ever want to do. It is often all that is needed.

8
THE POWER OF LOVE

In this introduction to healing I have concentrated on its practical ordinariness and played down its spiritual aspects, primarily because the word 'spiritual' is so emotive. Too often it is associated with, on the one hand, floaty ectoplasms or, on the other hand, narrow religious dogmas, neither of which has much relevance to healing. The real meaning of the concept goes far beyond clairvoyant experiences or religious differences. It transcends belief systems. It is our connection with the infinite, however you wish to interpret that. I am concerned about alienating those who would immediately dismiss healing as all hogwash, but I certainly don't want to disown the spiritual altogether.

'I'm happy calling it spiritual healing,' said one healer who works together with a doctor in general practice, 'because it is so much bigger and more wonderful than anything I could do on my own and also because it works on so many levels. I haven't seen any instant miracle cures, but I have seen diseases gradually go away as a person receives spiritual healing for their emotional pain, their loneliness, their lack of purpose.'

The complaint for which a patient comes to see the doctor or healer is rarely the whole story. One doctor said to me that a very high percentage of the patients who come to see him, perhaps as many as half, don't really want to get better. Illness has become a substitute for life.

This state of emptiness and sadness has been described as a sort of spiritual hunger or deprivation. It leaves us feeling separated from the whole, exiled, lost. In this context, healing can be seen as a sort of spiritual nourishment. It touches and awakens the 'inner healer' while at the same time it is a hotline to the source. Some people call this God. Make of it what you will. A healer tries to 'bring the healing through', as another healer put it, to affect *all* levels of a person, both seen and unseen and all in an atmosphere of non-judgemental acceptance. Trusting that the person's 'higher self', the divine spark, the God within, will be warmed and encouraged by the spiritual 'jump leads' is a very important part of the process. I don't talk about this much when I am healing unless the person I am working with brings it up and yet it informs everything I do.

Dr Craig Brown is a general practitioner who works with a healer. He has been developing what he calls 'spiritual diagnosis', bringing this extra dimension into his consulting room. 'A spiritual diagnosis is usually at a deeper level,' he says. 'And I try to "tune in" to the patient and listen very carefully for any clues, so that I can pick up what's going on behind the symptoms he is presenting.

'For example, a patient may visit my office to change his tablets for arthritis as the present ones are not helping. It may emerge that he is resentful of the way he was dismissed from his job twenty years ago, and shortly afterwards developed arthritis. The spiritual diagnosis may be one of *resentment*, but telling him this may not help. What does seem to help is the doctor grasping the essential core of the illness. Then by bringing the opposite and positive quality, such as forgiveness, into oneself as a therapist, this seems to initiate the healing process. I have often seen that this is all that is needed, and can by-pass years of psychoanalysis and counselling. By letting go of the past, bringing the person into the present, they can begin their own healing process.'

Dr Brown says that it became apparent to him once he started to think in this way that very often the essential nature of the problem in the spiritual diagnosis is fear: fear of illness, fear of old age, fear of lonelines, fear of death. 'The opposite quality to fear is love,' he says, 'and this really means the compassionate open-hearted love of all things. By simply adopting a sincere attitude of compassion we can heal our patients.'

When you start thinking about healing and health in these broader, more spiritual terms, the idea of 'success' or 'failure' becomes irrelevant. We're not just talking about physical symptoms anymore, but about a journey towards wholeness. As Penny Brohn says in her book *The Bristol Programme,* '... every step we take is another step towards understanding; every step brings us nearer to enlightenment. We may or we may not subdue the sickness in our physical body and alter its behaviour according to our wishes; we may rejoice in achieving that or let it go as an objective. In the end we shall be journeying for its own sake, not to reach a specific destination. All travellers always arrive eventually.' Healing may well start with the simple heartfelt desire to make something better, but it is really the beginning of a quest and an adventure that inevitably leads into metaphysical realms because ultimately it is a journey of transformation.

In this chapter I would like to return to the idea of feeling confident about offering this heart-to-heart resuscitation and some of the different areas where you might be glad to have it up your sleeve, so to speak. Don't worry about being inexperienced. Everybody has to start somewhere. There is an old Zen saying: 'In the beginner's mind there are many opportunities, in the expert's there are few.'

As some people are a little wary of the idea of healing, there is no need to call it that if it doesn't seem appropriate. When I worked as a volunteer in a hospice for cancer patients I often called it a 'foot massage' or 'a facial' or 'a little bit of lotion for your dry skin'. The difference comes with the quality of your intention – clear, focussed, loving. You've got to do it with all your heart.

SOME STORIES ABOUT HEALING

The fractious baby
My friend, Amelia Auckett, is an Australian nursing sister from Melbourne who teaches baby massage as an alter-

native to using drugs for unsettled and 'colicky' babies. In her Infant Welfare Clinic she became increasingly aware of the *mothers'* own needs for nurturing. 'Some of them didn't even know the meaning of the word,' she said. 'They would admit, yes, of course they liked to be held, but they wouldn't *ask* anybody. They'd never just ask their husbands to hold them, to touch them lovingly. So much of the touching that's done in Western society, certainly in Australia, is essentially sexual or has sexual overtones. They were afraid that a request for a hug would be misinterpreted. What I'm teaching people to do is to touch each other in an unconditional, loving, healing way. No sexual strings attached. I work in a very conservative profession so I have to be careful not to come across as weird. I don't go on about "energy" or "love" but that's what's really going on. For massage, read healing.'

She started by giving mothers a head and shoulder massage, using a very light touch. Many of them said, 'I wish my husband was here so you could show him how to do it', so she started holding classes at weekends so husbands could come too. The classes were enormously popular. Amelia found that once she'd introduced the idea that it was all right for men to give gentle healing massage to their wives and to receive it themselves in return, even the traditional tough, macho Aussie males responded enthusiastically.

'Asking for what you need is part of what I teach,' says Amelia. 'You can't just expect someone to *know* that you need a massage or a hug. A lot of women have a problem with this – they expect men to be mind readers. They hope someone will notice their needs, but don't speak up for themselves. Then, of course, they feel resentful, misunderstood, unloved or rejected.'

Amelia has given a lot of thought to the quality of these exchanges. 'There's a lot more than touching involved here,' she says. 'It's a deep sharing and it's unconditional love. It's a meeting of souls. I go within myself until I feel I'm really in touch with my own spirit, my own loving, then I can reach out and touch another with love. It's important to have that love of self. You can't truly love anyone else until you love yourself – your own God-self I call it.'

In our culture even something as natural as baby massage, which is done by mothers and grandmothers in most countries of the world, has become an area of no confidence. Amelia observed that when she encouraged mothers to try it, their babies cried less, fed better, slept better. 'It breaks the anxiety/pain cycle, it improves digestion and circulation, it creates emotional closeness and trust and is a positive way of giving attention.' (See Fig. 28.)

One very anxious young mother in Amelia's post-natal group suffered badly from post-natal blues. She was very depressed and apathetic, always scared of doing the wrong thing and harming the baby. Her baby cried a lot with 'colic' and had been given drugs to settle him. It was a vicious circle. The more worked up she got, the more the baby cried, the less sleep she and her husband got, the more hopeless the situation seemed. Amelia gave her some gentle healing massage and suggested that she have some aromatherapy from a professional along with some back and neck massages from her husband. Through being nurtured in this way, the young mother was able to learn by example how to massage her baby to their mutual pleasure and satisfaction. It gave her something positive to do for her baby and it calmed them both.

The young mother's comment was: 'I feel as if I have touched something very delicate. It's beautiful. We become one. My baby is now 19 months old and whenever I run my hands over his little body he smiles with pleasure. This, I feel, is a great gift he has received for life, for he is now a responsive, lovable, affectionate human being. Massage has played an important role. We prefer to use that now instead of medicines to calm him down after he has been upset.'

Amelia was asked one day to give a workshop for the staff at a school for the blind. She noticed a tiny, under-sized, deaf, mute, and blind two-year-old and said she'd like to demonstrate on him. They weren't too keen, saying

Fig. 28 Baby massage – a wonderful way to create emotional closeness and trust

he didn't respond well to strangers and was very disturbed, but she persuaded them to let her try.

'I sat him on my lap and just held him and loved him with all my heart,' she said. 'I communicated to him non-verbally that I wanted to give him a massage and share this love with him. I started very gently on his head and back and he wriggled his shoulders with pleasure. Then I did his arms and legs and face. When I finished, he just reached out and patted me on the cheek. It was so lovely – as if he was saying, "Thank you, that was beautiful."'

A few months later when Amelia followed it up, the staff had been incorporating a daily healing massage for this little boy and there was a lot of improvement in his behaviour, and in the relationship between him and his parents and grandparents. No more agonizing screaming fits and temper tantrums. They now felt they had a way to communicate with him. They had started to have him home for the weekends and were no longer sure they wanted to leave him in an institution for the rest of his life.

Massage and healing have a special place in the care of physically disabled and mentally handicapped children – anyone, in fact, who is likely to be left out of the world of communication. It has also been used very successfully in the care of premature babies, reducing the stressful effects of enforced separation from the mother or of frightening or painful medical procedures. Massage can also be particularly useful in helping to establish a bond between an adopted baby and its new parents.

My youngest child is adopted. She was born with a crippling bone disease and has spent much of her young life in the hospital having some pretty fearful treatments including surgery to straighten her twisted legs. I stayed with her and gave her healing every day at the hospital while her legs were in plaster and the medical team were delighted by how quickly and how well the bones healed. She is now walking, running, riding a bicycle and doing gymnastics. Apart from these obvious benefits, even more important was the bond of closeness that was created between us, often quite difficult to establish when you adopt an older child (she was ten years old when she came to live with us). Now if ever she gets any pain she comes and asks for healing and we sit together in a cocoon of warmth and closeness. Sometimes I massage her legs using a massage oil containing a few drops of essential oils (lavender, geranium and ginger, which is good for bone pain). Sometimes I just lay my hands on her hips, knees or feet and channel energy. It always makes a difference.

Of course, the logical extension of all this is to begin even before a baby is born. Many couples have discovered this unique act of joyous anticipation, where the father can enhance his feeling of closeness and participation by giving a gentle, healing massage to his wife during the pregnancy and also to his unborn child in the womb.

'You can teach love only by loving,' says Amelia. 'And you can learn about love only by experiencing it. If children are going to grow up to be loving adults, they have to learn about love right from the start. That early massage is the deepest expression of love. We've all got that love within us, all we have to do is tap into it and bring it through.'

Helping an elderly person

Many elderly people, especially if they live alone, may not have been touched in a loving way for years and years. I personally believe that this physical deprivation is the root cause of much ill health in the first place and a problem which our society hasn't even begun to tackle. The increased feeling of well-being from a gentle laying-on-of-hands healing or massage has the effect of reducing pain and therefore, possibly, the person may have less need for strong medication. People feel relief from headaches, constipation, joint pains, indigestion, insomnia and breathlessness.

It is wonderful to see how the beneficial effects of warm physical human contact begin to wrok almost immediately. The person becomes more relaxed, the breathing becomes less rapid and shallow, blood pressure becomes

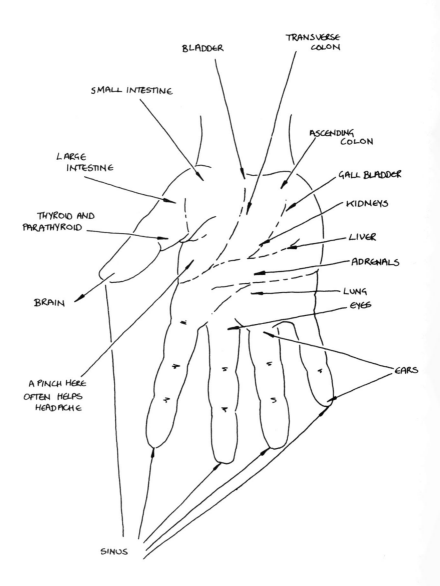

Fig. 28 Principal reflex points on the hands

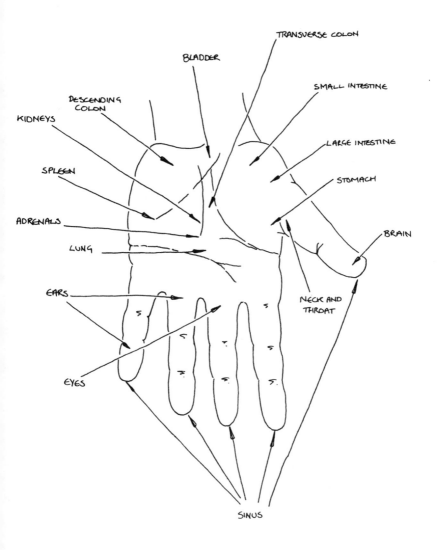

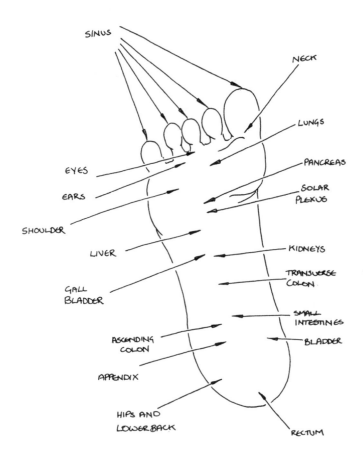

Fig. 29 Principal reflex points on the feet

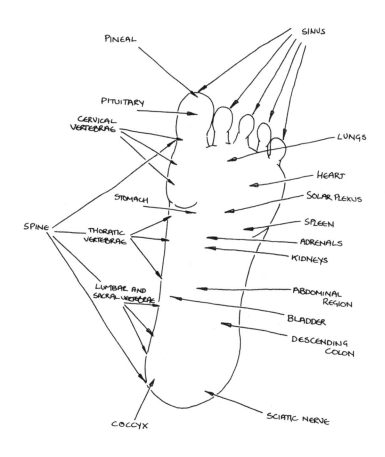

PINEAL

SINUS

PITUITARY

CERVICAL
VERTEBRAE

LUNGS

HEART

STOMACH

SOLAR PLEXUS

SPINE

THORATIC
VERTEBRAE

SPLEEN

ADRENALS

KIDNEYS

LUMBAR AND
SACRAL VERTEBRAE

ABDOMINAL
REGION

BLADDER

DESCENDING
COLON

COCCYX

SCIATIC NERVE

lower, heart rate slower. A few drops of aromatherapy oil bring instant relief from dry flaky skin, poor circulation and bed sores. Aching bones and muscles feel better; swelling is reduced. The input of loving energy makes a person feel less lonely, frightened or isolated – more accepted and accepting. Having a healing, a hand massage, a foot massage or a facial stimulates easy conversation and is a great reliever of boredom.

If the elderly person also happens to be a relative it is wonderful to have something so positive to do for her. It can break down barriers of non-communication and clear up years of 'unfinished business' in an atmosphere of love and gentleness.

In the psycho-geriatric where I was once a volunteer, one of the patients was a deaf old man called Ron. Dealing with deafness is a tricky problem. It's very difficult to behave normally towards a person when you are yelling at the top of your lungs. Everybody shouted at him – 'ALL RIGHT DEAR?' or 'HOW ARE WE TODAY?' or 'ARE YOU GOING TO EAT YOUR DINNER LIKE A GOOD BOY?' – and he just sat and stared out on the world like a visitor from another planet and nodded his head.

Ron didn't want to eat his dinner like a good boy. He didn't want to do anything much. He looked into the middle distance and occasionally shredded up a tissue into a thousand snowflakes and watched them fall to the ground. The staff all thought he was demented and nobody ever came to visit him. He'd been there for years.

One day I went and sat by his chair and held his hand. I didn't say anything but just looked at him and smiled. I wondered who he was and what he had seen in his long life. I tried to see him as he might have been – an athlete, a young lover, a father, a war hero. I felt very moved by his frailty and his predicament, isolated from the world of sound, cut off from communication, adrift like a castaway. I suddenly knew that the whole person was in there somewhere and that my heart could reach out from a place of total acceptance and touch his.

I stroked his cheek and he turned to look straight into my eyes. It was a moment of pure communication, a meeting of souls on our journey. That was all that happened, but I knew that he knew that I knew, and nothing more needed to be done.

Reflexology

One of the loveliest and most comforting ways to give healing to an elderly person is via reflexology on the hands and feet – an ancient art practised by the Chinese and probably the Egyptians too. To become a fully qualified reflexologist requires a proper course of study, but a knowledge of the principal points can be really helpful. Reflexology, or zone therapy, is a system of healing which sees the hands and particulary the feet as maps of the rest of the body. Like so many of the contemporary therapies that have an indisputable effect (acupuncture, shiatsu, etc.), *how* it works remains something of an enigma and is most likely to do with the circulation of energy currents in the body. Pressure or stimulation of particular points can reduce pain and break down congestion in the organs to which the areas relate (see Figs. 28 and 29).

The massage is usually done by supporting the foot with one hand and pressing with the tip of the other thumb on the relevant reflex points. It shouldn't be at all ticklish if your movements are firm and confident. I like to begin by quietly holding the foot in both my hands and pressing with both thumbs on the solar plexus reflex point for a minute or so. This has the effect of relaxing and calming the person so that the treatment which follows will be even more beneficial.

Some people prefer to work solely on the spinal reflex along the inside edge of the foot. This is the basis of the metamorphic technique which has a wonderful effect on the whole nervous system. (For more information, see booklist at the end.)

Helping someone who is dying

Everything I have learned about healing has helped me

work with the dying. I have learned that healing is not necessarily the same thing as cure and has more to do with quality of life. A friend of mine who died of AIDS said to me shortly before his death, 'I realize that my illness presents me with a choice. Either to be a helpless, hopeless victim dying of AIDS or to make my life right now what it always ought to have been.' He made peace with himself, took care of his 'unfinished business' with his family and chose to die at home surrounded by loving friends who looked after him with great care and gentleness till the end. People can be healed into death.

Looking back on it now I actually feel my own cancer was a gift helping me to see that every moment I live is precious and that death is not the enemy – fear is. 'Live each day as if it were your last,' said my inner voice, 'and death will fit into the scheme of things more easily when it comes.' In trying to understand how to live more comfortably and less fearfully with notions of death I think we probably learn a lot more about life and the value of living in the present moment.

As a healer, you can always help to create that safe space where dynamic change can take place whether a person has many years of life still to lead or only a few days. After all death is the most dynamic change that can happen to any of us and it will happen to all of us sometime. It is the only sure thing we share, apart from birth, with every other human being on this planet.

So how can we be helpful to people who are dying and give them hope when the doctors say their condition is terminal? As Stephen Levine says, 'Often when we speak of healing the question is asked, "How do we know when to stop healing and begin to prepare for death?" The question comes from a partial understanding. In reality, the opening to healing and the preparation for death are the same . . . they are aspects of a single whole.'

The most important thing is not to let your own fears or feelings of awkwardness and inadequacy intrude. Trying to 'cheer them up' or pretend they are going to be just fine is more about your needs than theirs. Somebody once called this 'the horse on the dining room table syndrome' – everyone knows it's there but nobody likes to mention it. This doesn't mean you have to keep on pointing it out. Just gently let it be known that it's all right to talk about any worries, doubts or fears or anything else for that matter. It's also all right not to talk at all. The choice is theirs. You are just the facilitator. Act normally! It's still the same person inside the dying body. You can give them healing without letting yourself get attached to the results. The energy will go to where it is most needed and help them with their transformation. All you have to take to a dying person is yourself and your open heart. If you come with fear, guilt, advice or self-righteousness you will not be a safe place. If you come with stillness and compassion you will be a channel through which healing energy can flow.

Stephen Levine's beautiful book, *Who Dies?*, is full of ideas about how to make a dying person's last days comfortable, peaceful and companionable while he or she prepares for the last great adventure. You can stand steady with someone while they face the unknown. You can sit in loving kindness, accompanying a person on the last pilgrimage. You are allowing a balance to occur by being in balance yourself.

The next generation

Little children are usually very interested in healing and show a great natural aptitude. They have wonderful imaginations and spontaneous loving hearts. They are not surprised by magic. Encourage them to be plant and animal healers, let them massage the baby, show them how to take granny's headache away and it will become a way of life.

FURTHER READING

Beaulieu, John, *Music and Sound in the Healing Arts*, Station Hill Press, New York, 1987.

Brennan, Barbara Ann, *Hands of Light*, Bantam/New Age, New York, 1986.

Brohn, Penny, *The Bristol Programme*, Century, London, 1987.

Cade, Maxwell C. and Nona Coxhead, *The Awakened Mind*, Wildwood, Hounslow, 1979.

Chopra, Deepak, *Quantum Healing*, Bantam, New York, 1989.

Copland, Don, *So You Want to be a Healer?*, NFSH, Sunbury on Thames, 1981.

Dass, Ram and Paul Gorman, *How Can I Help?*, Rider, London, 1985.

Eastcott, Michal *The Silent Path*, Rider, London, 1969.

Elliott, Rose, *The Green Age Diet*, Fontana/Collins, London, 1990.

Feild, Reshad, *Here to Heal*, Element Books, Shaftesbury, 1985.

Ferrucci, Piero, *What We May Be*, Turnstone Press, Wellingborough, 1982.

Garfield, Laeh Maggie, *Sound Medicine*, Celestial Arts, Berkeley, 1987.

Gawler, Ian, *You Can Conquer Cancer*, Hill of Content, Melbourne, 1984.

Gerber, Richard, *Vibrational Medicine*, Bear & Co., Santa Fe, 1988.

Gore, Anya, *Reflexology*, Optima, London, 1990.

Hodgkinson, Liz, *Spiritual Healing*, Piatkus, London, 1990.

Holbeche, Soozi, *The Power of Gems and Crystals*, Piatkus, London, 1989.

Horstmann, Lorna, *A Handbook of Healing*, NFSH, Sunbury on Thames.

Jackson, Judith, *Aromatherapy*, Dorling Kindersley, London, 1987.

Jampolsky, Gerald G., *Out of Darkness, Into The Light*, Bantam, New York, 1989.

Joy, W. Brugh, *Joy's Way*, J.P. Tarcher Inc., Los Angeles, 1979.

Kaptchuk, Ted and Michael Croucher, *The Healing Arts*, BBC, London, 1986.

Krieger, Dolores, *The Therapeutic Touch*, Prentice Hall, New York, 1986.

Krieger, Dolores, *Living the Therapeutic Touch*, Dodd, Mead and Co., New York, 1987.

Kubler-Ross, Elisabeth, *On Death and Dying*, Tavistock Publications, London, 1970.

Kubler-Ross, Elisabeth, *Death: The Final Stage of Growth*, Prentice Hall, New Jersey, 1975.

Levine, Stephen, *Who Dies?* Anchor Books, New York, 1982.

MacManaway, Bruce and Johanna Turcan, *Healing*, Thorsons, Wellingborough, 1983.

Macrae, Janet, *Therapeutic Touch*, Arkana, London, 1987.

Mansfield, Peter, *The Good Health Handbook*, Grafton, London, 1988.

Markides, Kyriacos, *The Magus of Strovolos*, Arkana, London, 1985.

Moss, Richard, *How Shall I Live?*, Celestial Arts, Berkeley, 1985.

Peck, M. Scott, *The Road Less Travelled*, Touchstone, New York, 1978.

Price, Shirley, *Practical Aromatherapy*, Thorsons, Wellingborough, 1983.

Pullar, Philippa, *Spiritual and Lay Healing*, Penguin, London, 1988.

Roet, Brian, *All in The Mind? – Think Yourself Better*, Optima, London, 1987.

Roose-Evans, James, *Inner Journey, Outer Journey*, Rider, London, 1987.

Russell, Peter, *The T.M. Technique*, RKP, London, 1976.

Saint-Pierre, Gaston and Debbie Boater, *The*

Metamorphic Technique, Element Books, Tilsbury, 1982.

Schwartz, Jack, *Human Energy Systems*, E.P. Dutton, New York, 1980.

Siegel, Bernie S., *Love, Medicine and Miracles*, Rider, London, 1986.

Smith, Erica and Nicholas Wilks, *Meditation*, Optima, London, 1988.

Stephenson, James H., *Helping Yourself With Homoeopathic Remedies*, Thorsons, Wellingborough, 1976.

Stevens Chris, *Alexander Technique*, Optima, London, 1987.

Taylor, Allegra, *I Fly Out With Bright Feathers – The Quest of a Novice Healer*, Fontana/Collins, London, 1987.

Taylor, Allegra, *Acquainted With the Night – A Year on the Frontiers of Death*, Fontana/Collins, London, 1989.

Tisserand, Robert, *The Art of Aromatherapy*, C.W. Daniel and Co. Ltd, Saffron Walden, 1977.

Watson, Andrew, and Nevill Drury, *Healing Music*, Prism Press, Bridport, 1987.

Weiner, Michael A., *Maximum Immunity: How to fortify your natural defences against Cancer, AIDS, Arthritis, Allergies and other immune deficiency diseases*, Gateway, Bath, 1986.

Wilson Annie and Lilla Bek, *What Colour Are You?*, Turnstone Press, Wellingborough, 1981.

INDEX

Page numbers in *italic* refer to the illustrations

abdominal chakra, *29*, 30, 67
Aborigines, 1, 60–1, 73
absent healing, 19, *20*, 69
acupuncture, 26–7
addiction, 87
adopted children, 124–5
adrenalin, 30, 93–4
Africa, 74, 76
AIDS, 132
ailments, 97–117
Albinoni, Tommaso, 83
Alexander Technique, 106
alexandrite, 69
alpha rhythm, 22, 23
amber, 67
American Indians, 1, 42
amethysts, 69
amino acids, 92
animal protein, 89
animals, symbols, 42
anxiety, 75, *76*
aquamarine, 69
aromatherapy, 70–2
arthritis, 101–2, 119
asthma, 75
Aswad, 84
Auckett, Amelia, 120–4, 125
auras, 26, 27, 47, 49, 108
Australia, 1, 61, 73, 76
autistic children, 79–80
auto-immune system, 56
auto-suggestion, 7
Autolycus, 75

baby massage, 120–1, *121*,
    122–5
Bach, J.S., 76, 83
Bach flower remedies, 28, 98,
    112–15
backache, 78, 105–7
Barber, Samuel, 83
base chakra, *29*, 30, 67
bean curd, 92

Beethoven, Ludwig van, 78,
    79–80, 83
Benor, Dr Daniel, 7
bereavement, 107
bergamot, essential oil, 71
beta rhythm, 22, 23
beverages, 91
Bible, 1, 75
biofeedback, 22
bioelectrical energy, 3
biomagnetic energy, 3
blood, haemoglobin, 2
blood pressure, 24, 75, 95
bloodstone, 67
blue: colour visualization
    breathing, 103; gemstones, 69
bone healing, 110, *110, 111*
Brahms, Johannes, 83, 105
brain: hemispheres, *63*, 64;
    limbic system 70; meditation
    94, 95; waves, 22–3
breathing: colour visualization
    breathing, 103–4, *104*;
    humming meditation, 79;
    meditation, 96; techniques,
    22–3; visualization, 34–5
breathlessness, 125
Bristol Cancer Help Centre, 90
Brohn, Penny, 120
brow chakra, *29*, 31, 69
Brown, Dr Craig, 119–20
Bruckner, Anton, 83
Bruyere, Rosalyn, 56
Buddhism, 31, 93
Bulgaria, 80
Byrd, William, 85

caffeine, 89
cancer, 10–11, 35, 43, 86–7, 132
carbohydrates, 89
cardio-vascular disease, 4
castor oil packs, 101–2, *102*
Catholic Church, 31

caves, visualization, 36–7
cells, 97–8
centring, 49
chakras, 18, 26–7, 28–32, *29*;
  balancing with crystal
  healing, 67, *68*; Energy
  Spiral, 49, *50*; gemstones
  and, 67–9; and humming,
  75–6, 79
chanting, 74, 75, 85
ch'i, 11–12
Child, Pose of a, 105, *105*, 106
children, 133; autistic, 79–80;
  baby massage, 120–1, *121*,
  122–5; comfort healing, 107;
  imagination, 33; legislation,
  99
China, 1, 11–12, 92, 131
Christianity, 13, 14, 31
Church, 13, 14
Churches Council for Health
  and Healing, 14
Churchill, Sir Winston, 86
circle dancing, 80
citrine, 69
clairvoyance, 27
cleansing crystals, 62
closing energy spiral, *57*, 58
coffee enemas, 88
colonic irrigation, 88
colour: chakras, 27, 28, 32;
  colour visualization
  breathing, 103–4, *104*;
  gemstones, 67–9;
  visualization, 34–5
comfort healing, 107–8, *108*
commitment, 86, 88
compassion, 44
concern, excessive, Bach flower
  remedy, 115
Confederation of Healing
  Organizations, 14, 99
consciousness, 8–9, 22
constipation, 125
consultations, 16–21
costs, 14–15
counselling, 14, 16
Creation myths, 73
Croucher, Michael, 12
crown chakra, *29*, 31, 69

Crutcher, Rusty, 84
crying, 111–12
crystals, 28, 60–70; absent
  healing, 69; balancing
  chakras, 67, *68*; bone
  healing, 110, *111*; choosing,
  61–2; dowsing with, 65, *66*;
  energy grid, 65, *65*; gem
  elixirs, 62; healing with,
  65–7; meditation with, 62–5;
  re-energizing with, 64, *64*;
  taking out pain with, 105–6,
  106

dairy products, 91
dance meditation, 80–2
dancing, 74, 75
David, King of Israel, 75
Davis, Miles, 85
deafness, 130
death, 131–3
Debussy, Claude Achille, 83
delta rhythm, 23
depression, 9, 24
despondency, Bach flower
  remedy, 114–15
detoxification, 87–90
diamonds, 69
didgeridoo, 76, 110
diet, 86–92
digestive system, detoxification,
  87–90
distant healing, 19, *20*, 69
divination, 65
doctors, 13, 15, 97, 99
dowsing, 62, 65, *66*
'drawing off' pain, 56
drumming, 76
Dvorak, Antonin, 76, 83
dying, 131–3

eating habits, 86–7
Edwards, Harry, 44
eggs, 91
Egypt, 1, 80, 131
elderly people, 125–31
Elgar, Edward, 83
elixirs, gem, 62, 67
emeralds, 69
Emerson, Ralph Waldo, 35

emotional problems, 16, 24, 107, 111–12
enemas, 88
energeia, 6
energy: auras, 26, 27; balancing exercise, 54–6; chakras, 26–7, 28–32, *29*; crystals, 62, 64; diet and, 89; experiencing, 46–7, *46*; feeling the flow, 47–58; getting in touch with, *48*, 49; healthy body, 87; life-force, 11–12;; listening meditation, 78; and matter, 27–8, 59; re-energizing, 64, *64*; visualization, 47–9
energy grid, 65, *65*
Energy Spiral, 49–51 *50*; closing, *57*, 58
Enigma, 84
Enya, 84
essential oils, 70–2
exercise, 90–3

faith healing, 1, 5
farming, 89
Fauré, Gabriel, 78, 84
fear, 2, 113, 119
feet: humming meditation, 76; massage, 79–80; reflex points, *128–9*, 131
Ferrucci, Piero, 41, 77
Festival of Mind, Body and Spirit, 2
fibre, 89
fire opals, 67
firehose, visualization, 47–9
first aid, 56
fish, 91
Fitzgerald, Scott, 84
'flash tasks', visualization, 33, *34*
flowers: Bach flower remedies, 28, 98, 112–15; visualization, 38–41
fluorite, 69
Flying Monkey Orchestra, 84
folk medicine, 1–2
food additives, 89
fruit, 91

Garfield, Laeh Maggie, 86
garnets, 67, 69
Gawler, Ian, 88
gem elixirs, 62, 67
gemstones, 67–9
General Medical Council, 13
geranium, essential oil, 72
Gerber, Dr Richard, 27, 61, 72
Getz, Stan, 85
Gilberto, 85
God, 119
grains, 91
grape mono-diet, 88
Greece, 1
green: colour visualization breathing, 103; gemstones, 69
Gregorian chants, 85
Groeschel, Gene, 84
'grounding', 37
guitars, 76
Gypsy Kings, 85
Gyuto Monks, 84

haemoglobin, 2
halos, 31
Handel, George Friderick, 83
hands: feeling energy, 46–7, *46*; reflex points, *126–7*, 131
harmony, 77–8, 80
Harperbury Hospital, 74–5
headaches, 24, 125; tension, 99–101, *100*
healers: absent healing, 19, *20*; contacting, 14; costs, 14–15; developing your own powers, 43–58; first consultation, 16–21; length of session, 21; reactions to, 21–2
heart: chakra, *29*, 30–1, 69; disease, 4, 24; energy, 51, *52*, 53; humming and, 76
hemispheres, brain, *63*, 64
herbal tea, 99–101
herbalism, 28, 98
herbs, 91
high blood pressure, 24, 75
Hinduism, 11, 31
Holbeche, Soozi, 60
holistic approach, 8, 10–11, 74
home visits, 19

Homer, 75
homoeopathy, 28, 62, 98, 112, 115–17
homoeostasis, 87
Horn, Paul, 84
hospitals, 15, 19–21
humming, 75, 79–80
humpback whales, 24, 84
hypnosis, 35

images, mental, 7, 32–41, *34*, 47–9
imagination, 6, 33, 42, 97
immune system: detoxification and, 87; healing and, 2–3, 7, 56; illness and, 9; meditation and, 94, 95; and 'spontaneous remission', 97
Indian music, 84
Indians, American, 1, 42
indigestion, 125
indigo: colour visualization breathing, 104; gemstones, 69
'inner travel', 8
Inquisition, 13
insomnia, 125
interest, lack of, Bach flower remedy, 113–14
iron, 89
irrigation, colonic, 88

jade, 69
James, William, 8–9
Jesus Christ, 1, 4
joint pain, 24, 101–2, 125
Joy, Brugh, 51
juniper, essential oil, 72

Kaptchuk, Ted, 12
kidneys, 30, 78
knees, 76
Kobialka, Daniel, 84
Krieger, Dolores, 2

lapis lazuli, 69
Larkin, 85
Larkin, Philip, 3–4
lavender, essential oil, 71
laying-on-of-hands, 1
legislation, 98–9
Levine, Stephen, 132, 133

life-force, 9, 11–12, 70, 98
light bulbs, essential oil, 72
limbic system, 70
listening meditation, 77–9
loneliness, Bach flower remedy, 114
love, 4, 5–6, 44, 95, 98, 118–33
lullabies, 79
Lynch, James, 3

MacLaine, Shirley, 35
MacManaway, Bruce, 15
magenta, colour visualization breathing, 104
magnetic healing, 1
The Magus of Strovolos (Markides), 5
mantras, 74, 96
marjoram, essential oil, 71
Markides, Kyriacos C., 5
martial arts, 48
massage: aromatherapy, 70–2; baby massage, 120–5, *121*; elderly people, 125–31; foot, 79–80; reflexology, 131
matter: and energy, 27–8, 59; vibrations, 75
meat, 91
meditation, 93–6; crystals and, 62, 64–5; dance or movement, 80–2; humming, 79–80; listening, 77–9
mental images, 7, 32–41, *34*, 47–9
mental powers, 6–7
meridians, 12, 26–7
Metamorphic Technique, 131
metaphors, 41–2
mind, subconscious, 42
mineral supplements, 90
Moss, Richard, 5, 45, 82
movement meditation, 80–2
Moving Hearts, 84
Mozart, Wolfgang Amadeus, 76, 83
multiple sclerosis, 75
muscle pain, 24
music, 24, 72–85
myrrh, essential oil, 71
mysticism, 8–9

mythology, 73

National Federation of Spiritual Healers (NFSH), 2, 13, 14, 46
National Health Service, 15
neck, stiffness, 101
neroli, essential oil, 72
nerves, healing, 109
'New Age' healing methods, 28
New Testament, 6
nurses, 2, 15, 19
nuts, 91

Odyssey (Homer), 75
oils: cooking, 91; essential, 70–2
Oldman, Coyote, 84
opals, 67
orange: colour visualization breathing, 103; gemstones, 67
Orthodox Church, 76
oversensitivity, Bach flower remedy, 114
oxygen, haemoglobin, 2

Pachelbel, Johan, 83
pain: crystal healing, 65–7; 'drawing off', 56; joints, 24, 101–2, 125; tension headaches, 99–101, *100*
Palestrina, Giovanni Pierluigi da, 85
Paracelsus, 26
pendulums, dowsing, 65, *66*
peppermint, essential oil, 72
peridot, 69
pineal gland, 31, 64
placebo effect, 7, 97
plants: Bach flower remedies, 28, 98, 112–15; essential oils, 70
Pose of a Child, 105, *105*, 106
Prana, 11, 49
pregnancy, 125
processed foods, 89
protein, 89, 92
psychic healing, 1
Pullar, Philippa, 9
purple, gemstones, 69

quartz crystals, 60–1, 62, 67

Rachmaninov, Sergei, 84
Ravel, Maurice, 84
red: colour visualization breathing, 103; gemstones, 67
reflex points: feet, *128–9* hands, *126–7*
reflexology, 131
rejuvenation, 64
relaxation, 24; basic posture, 106, *107*; during healing, 21–2; and humming, 75–6, *76*
religion, 5, 7
remedies, 99–117
Remen, Rachel Naomi, 16
remission, 'spontaneous', 97
rescue remedy, Bach flower remedy, 115
Robson, Mark, 84
Rodriguez, Antonio, 85
Rome, 1
root chakra, 29, 30, 67
rose, essential oil, 72
rose quartz, 69
rosemary, essential oil, 72
rubies, 67
Russian Orthodox Church, 76

Sachdev, 84
sacral chakra, 29, 30, 67
sacred dance, 80
Sade, 84
salt, 89
Samuel, Book of, 75
sandalwood, essential oil, 72
sapphires, 69
Saul, 75
scar tissue, healing, 109
Schubert, Franz, 83
Schuessler, Dr William, 115
Schwartz, Jack, 22–3, 25, 103
seasonings, 91
self-healing, 9–11, 22, 24–5, 86
self-help groups, 14
senses: crystals, 60–70; dance or movement meditation, 80–5; music and sound, 72–80; smell, 70–2; touch, 59–60

sexuality, 121
Shiatsu massage, 26
shoulders, stiffness, 101
Sibelius, Jean, 84
Siegel, Bernie, 95, 97, 98
singing, 43
skin, touch, 18
smell, sense of, 70-2
Smith, Erica, 93
sodalite, 69
solar plexus, 76
solar plexus chakra, 29, 30, 69
soul, 4, 49
sound, 72-80, 110
Spence, Christopher, 111
spiritual growth, 86
spiritual healing, 1, 4-6, 118-19
spiritualism, 4
'spontaneous remission', 97
sprouts, 91
stagnant energy, 27, 28
Stearns, Michael, 84
Steel Pulse, 84
Steiner, Rudolph, 94-5
stiffness, neck and shoulders, 101
stomach disorders, 24
Stravinsky, Igor, 84
stress, 93-4
stress clinics, 22
subconscious mind, 42
sugar, 89
suggestion, 7
supplements, vitamin, 90
sweets, 91
symbols, 41-2

T'ai Chi, 92
tea, herbal, 99-101
tea tree, essential oil, 72
tears, 111-12
temple dancing, 80
tension, 24, 93-4
tension headaches, 99-101, 100
terraces of flowers, visualization, 38-41
therapeutic touch, 1, 2, 15
theta rhythm, 23
Third Eye, 69
thought, 7

throat chakra, 29, 31, 69
thymus gland, 30, 31
thyroid gland, 31
Tibet, 6
tissue salts, 115-17
tofu, 92
topaz, 67, 69
touch, 18, 28, 59-60, 121
tourmaline, 69
transcendental meditation (TM), 95-6
Transpersonal Point, 29, 31-2
trees, visualization, 37-8
trust, 6, 9
Truth, 41
turquoise: colour visualization breathing, 103; gemstones, 69

ultrasound, 73
Ulysses, 75
uncertainty, Bach flower remedy, 113
underwater sea cave, visualization, 36-7
universe, 72-3, 75

Vangelis, 84
vaporizers, essential oil, 72, 73
Vaughan Williams, Ralph, 84
vegetables, 92
vegetarian diet, 89
Verdi, Giuseppe, 83
vibracoustic therapy, 74-5
vibrational medicine, 59
vibrations: chakras, 28; crystals, 61; and matter, 59; sound, 72-5
violet, colour visualization breathing, 104
violins, 76
visualization , 32-41, 34; balancing chakras, 68; being a tree, 37-8; colour visualization breathing, 103-4, 104; crystals, 62-4; 'drawing off' pain, 56; feeling the flow of energy, 47-9; healing and, 7, 18; terraces of flowers, 38-41; underwater sea cave, 36-7

vitamin E oil, 109
vitamin supplements, 90
Vivaldi, Antonio, 83
Vogel, Marcel, 61, 67

Wagner, Richard, 83
water, humming under, 79
Weiner, Michael A., 90
whales, humpback, 24, 84
Wheater, Tim, 85
Wilks, Nicholas, 93

wine, 89
Winter, Paul, 85
witchcraft, 13
wulfenite, 67

yellow: colour visualization
    breathing, 103; gemstones, 69

Zen Buddhism, 120
zircon, 69
Zone Therapy, 131